Why is

GW00792447

So Good?

Aubrey Morris

www.apostolos-publishing.com

Why is God so Good? By Aubrey Morris

First Published in Great Britain in 2019

Faithbuilders, An Imprint of Apostolos Publishing Ltd,

3rd Floor, 207 Regent Street,

London W1B 3HH

www.apostolos-publishing.com

Copyright © 2019 Aubrey Morris

All rights reserved. No part of this book may be reproduced or transmitted in any form or by any means, electronic or mechanical, including photocopying, recording, or by any information storage and retrieval system, without permission in writing from the publisher.

Unless otherwise indicated, Scripture references are taken from THE HOLY BIBLE, NEW INTERNATIONAL VERSION®, NIV® Copyright © 1973, 1978, 1984, 2011 by Biblica, Inc.® Used by permission. All rights reserved worldwide. Scripture references marked "NKJV" are taken from the New King James Version®. Copyright © 1982 by Thomas Nelson. Used by permission. All rights reserved. Scripture quotations marked (TLB) are taken from The Living Bible copyright © 1971. Used by permission of Tyndale House Publishers, Inc., Carol Stream, Illinois 60188. All rights reserved. Scripture quotations marked MSG are taken from THE MESSAGE, copyright © 1993, 1994, 1995, 1996, 2000, 2001, 2002 by Eugene H. Peterson. Used by permission of NavPress. All rights reserved. Represented by Tyndale House Publishers, Inc. Scripture quotations marked (NLT) are taken from the Holy Bible, New Living Translation, copyright ©1996, 2004, 2015 by Tyndale House Foundation. Used by permission of Tyndale House Publishers, Inc., Carol Stream, Illinois 60188. All rights reserved.

British Library Cataloguing-in-Publication Data

A catalogue record for this book is available from the British Library.

ISBN: 978-1-912120-25-3

Cover Design by Faithbuilders | Image © Subbotina | Dreamstime.com. Author Photo by Levi Morris.

Printed and bound in Great Britain by Marston Book Services Limited, Oxfordshire.

DEDICATION

To Gail Teunissen, my first boss:

(Retired Principal of Addington Primary School)

You showed love, kindness and understanding. You gave me room to express the goodness of God towards the children in my own unique way.

Thank you for believing in me. You took a chance on me when I was fresh out of college, and it all turned out well.

You had that special touch as principal and friend. You will always be loved and treasured.

ACKNOWLEDGEMENTS

To my beautiful wife Auriel Haylene Morris; you are my treasure and God-given gift. I love you more now than ever before. Your belief in my potential inspires me. The Bible is true in calling you a good gift *(Proverbs 18:22)*.

To my sons Dillon and Levi; you bring joy to my heart. Keep God close, my sons. He will lead and guide you.

To my extended family and friends; I cherish and appreciate you all. Your names alone would fill this book if I began to pen them.

To Pastor Wayne Thring, my greatest mentor; thank you for leading me to Jesus. He is the greatest gift I could ever have received. Your father's heart and godly example spur me on in my love-walk with God.

Thank you to my editor, Brendan Marrett, for your initial exceptional editorial work on this project.

Thank you to Apostolos Publishers for believing in this project and helping me bring it to a finished product.

FOREWORD

When Aubrey asked me to do the foreword for his new book, *Why Is God So Good?* I must admit, he had me guessing. One of the thoughts resounding in my mind was, "Is it not obvious?" The common refrain "God is good all the time, and all the time God is good" possibly lulled me into a sense of thinking that we all knew why God is good.

This book jolted me out of my limited, comfortable thinking on the subject of the goodness of God. Line after line, Aubrey adds layer upon layer to his unpacking of the sometimes hidden yet ought-to-have-been-known truths about the goodness of our Father.

Aubrey has written an inspirational guide for those who want to know more about the goodness of God. The insights, personal experiences, and thought-provoking facets of a multi-faceted God kept me reading, and not wanting to put this book down.

We are taken on a pleasant journey, from understanding God's gifts of freewill and goodwill, to knowing the goodness of God in our dark moments, and concluding with coming to a place of rest, where we can celebrate and enjoy God's abundant goodness.

Showing the hallmarks of a great Bible teacher, Aubrey's appropriate use of Scripture references adds greater meaning and brings clarity to the content. I thoroughly enjoyed this read, and I know you will too, as you gain a greater insight into the goodness of our God.

Wayne Thring: Senior Pastor, Kingdom Connect Ministries (South Africa).

CONTENTS

=====================================

"O taste and see that the Lord is good: blessed are they that trust in Him."

Psalm 34:8

=====================================

INTRODUCTION

"Good" is a word we probably hear every day. A word can be used so frequently that we tend to see it as common and miss or nullify the full meaning and power of its reality. The GOOD that pertains to God is pure and unique. God is abundantly good. God is super-good. God is awesomely good. The Bible tells us that God's goodness is very rich (*Romans 2:4*).

Goodness is the very essence of God. When the Bible claims that God is good, it is saying is that God is:

1. PERFECT — flawless; there is no weakness or sin in Him;
2. UPRIGHT — righteous, holy and just;
3. KIND — a good Father and gentle comforter;
4. BENEVOLENT — overwhelmingly generous;
5. WHOLESOME — He heals, restores and satisfies;
6. GRACIOUS — He gives us what we do not deserve; and:
7. MERCIFUL — He forgives and does not punish us as we deserve.

Here are two verses from the Bible that ratify these seven of the many character traits of God:

"You are God, ready to pardon, gracious and merciful, slow to anger, abundant in kindness" (Nehemiah 9:17 NKJV).

"The LORD, The LORD, God, merciful and gracious, longsuffering, and abundant in goodness and truth" (Exodus 34:6 NKJV).

These verses clearly show that God is patient, loving, and not willing that we should perish. God is restorative and very compassionate.

The English meaning of the word "good" is fine, of high quality, profitable and virtuous. In Greek the equivalent word *kalos* means kindness, benevolence, humaneness. In Hebrew the equivalent word *ṭôb* means well, fair, pleasing, best, beauty, bountiful. The same meaning is conveyed in Genesis when God declared all He had created to be good, because it was pleasing to Him. It was right, perfect, and in harmony with His character and intent.

God is good because He is upright and just. God is good because He is virtuous, dignified and truthful. God is good because He is blameless, admirable and ultra-superior. God's goodness can never be tainted or overcome by evil. He cannot sin, and neither can He be tempted with evil.

On the other hand, Satan (the rebellious fallen archangel known as the Devil) cannot be good, nor do good acts, because he is evil in nature and purpose. Just as people tend to stay far away from scorpions because they possess a deadly sting – for it is in their nature to sting – it is in Satan's nature to carry out evil. Jesus called him *"the father of lies"* *(John 8:44)*. There is nothing good about Satan's agenda. Those who follow or worship him are doomed, unless they repent and choose Jesus.

God does not just possess goodness or carry out good acts. Rather, He is the personification of goodness. Similarly, we know that God does not just show love, but that He is LOVE. *1 John 4:7–8* says, *"Beloved, let us love one another: for love is of God … God is love" (NKJV)*. Goodness flows out of God's love. To say it another way, the God of love is good. Unlike Satan's, there is nothing evil about God's agenda. Those who follow and worship Him are guaranteed to be blessed and guaranteed a good end. God created us out of His love and goodness. Love and goodness are some of the major attributes that define Him. He is an approachable God, even though He is majestic and seated on high. He sent Jesus to die for us so we could be reconciled to Him, and thereby enjoy close fellowship with Him. He is not hiding from us. He shows kindness and concern for mankind. *Psalm 138:6* says, *"Though the Lord is exalted, He looks kindly on the lowly" (NIV)*.

Because God is good, we can trust in His love and kindness. Because God is good, we can trust in His mercy, grace and generosity. We can trust in His power and protection and take Him at His Word that we have a hopeful future. In *Jeremiah 29:11* God said, *"For I know the thoughts that I think toward you…, thoughts of peace and not evil, to give you a future and hope" (NKJV)*.

Mankind ought to be running to God, not from Him. He has never failed anyone. He has never led anyone into evil or damnation. He is known as a God who provides a way of escape *(1 Corinthians 10:13)*. He has good plans for our lives. He has paths of righteousness, if we would only follow Him. God leads us by love, not by intimidation and wrath. He meted out His wrath for our sins on Jesus on the cross. It is God's goodness that leads men and women to repentance *(Romans 2:4)*. God brings good into the situations we face.

When Moses desired God to show him His glory, God made all His goodness pass before him *(Exodus 33:19)*. This shows us that the most glorious thing about God is that He is absolutely GOOD! We always desire to show others our best side, our best achievements and our best performance. God's best side or best performance, so to speak, is His goodness. This is not to take away from His glorious power, wonder and beauty.

I know that the world is full of suffering and violent atrocities, but if we look around and observe carefully, we will see there is still goodness on the earth. *Psalm 33:5* says, *"He loves righteousness and justice; The earth is full of the goodness of the LORD" (NKJV)*. God's goodness is functional, not ornamental. In other words, God is not good just by name or title. His goodness is workable and usable. It brings about change. He is able to bring or turn our bad situations into good. God wants us to partner with Him by taking on His good nature and spread goodness in the world.

Some people question the realty of God's goodness, especially when faced with adverse situations or experiences. We cannot just decide to blame God and see Him as devoid of empathy and goodness because we had a bad day or because we experienced some tragic event. God's goodness is not determined by our experiences. Rather, God's goodness is determined or defined by His character.

The Bible says that Jesus is touched by our troubles. He is concerned and understands what we go through. Hebrews 4:15 says, *"For we do not have a High Priest [Jesus Christ] who cannot sympathize with our weakness, but was in all points tempted as we are, yet without sin" (NKJV)*. God is kind enough to spread His goodness our way, and not just keep it to Himself. God is not good just to some, but to all. Psalm 145:9 says, *"The Lord is good to all: and His tender mercies are over all His works" (NKJV)*.

Even as flawed human beings, there is still goodness in us. We see it in how we love and care for others. We see it displayed by doctors and nurses in hospitals towards their patients. We see it displayed by teachers in their classrooms and by mothers towards their children. We see it in people who adopt children and give them a home, and in those who leave their countries to serve people in foreign places.

I am thinking of Mother Teresa here. She sacrificed many of her own comforts to love and care for the unlovable and poor people in

Calcutta. She established hospice centres for the blind, aged and disabled and also helped the lepers. Certainly, there are many more who have displayed a great labour of love towards others.

If you have lived long enough, you have surely realized that the world is filled with tragic and heart-breaking atrocities and sufferings. In the midst of such tragedies and injustices, God is still good, and He will one day right the wrongs. *Revelation 21* speaks of a time when God will wipe away every tear. He will rid the world of sickness, pain, death and poverty. There will be no crime and no fear. God Himself will dwell with mankind. For now, our job is to allow God's goodness to flow through us to others. God designed us to exude goodness. It is not an attribute reserved only for Himself. When God's attributes are truly and purposefully lived out by us, the world becomes a better place.

This goodness we have in us has a source — God. After all we are made in His image and likeness *(Genesis 1:26)*. Although we are not God, we possess many of His traits. Unfortunately, because of sin, our goodness can be overshadowed or tainted by things such as hatred, bitterness, pride, selfishness, lust and envy, or we can sometimes withhold the goodness we ought to do when we feel hurt, angry, betrayed or discouraged. The Bible says, *"Withhold not good from those to whom it is due, When it is in the power of your hand to do so" (Proverbs 3:27 NKJV)*. Joseph could have withheld the good he was able to do for his brothers based on the cruel treatment they had meted out to him in his youth. Instead, he chose to forgive them and bless them in many practical ways. It was not an easy choice, after he had suffered the pain of rejection from his brothers and the lonely years without his father.

God does not fluctuate in being good. He is not good one day and then evil the next. In this way, He is very predictable, meaning you can expect Him to be good — everyday. The Bible tells us that God's mercies are new every morning *(Lamentations 3:22–23)*. He tells us in the book of Malachi that He does not change *(Malachi 3:6)*. I am glad that God is constant as this shows He can be trusted.

Another facet to God's personality is that He is the BOSS — and will always be. We ought to love being under Him. He rebukes us when we are wrong, but also restores us so we will not perish. He deals with us in love. He never abuses us or treats us cruelly, for cruelty and neglect are not in His nature. No one really wants a boss who is cruel and abusive. People may abandon or disown us, but God will always accept us. It is good for us to learn about God's goodness and to experience it. It is a cushion against the many harsh realities we face. He desires for us to be aware of His goodness. God is the perfect role model when it comes to goodness. He wants us to trust in His goodness. He is the One who defines what is right and what is pleasing.

We thrive on God's goodness, when we understand and embrace it. There are people who do not acknowledge God's goodness, yet they benefit daily from it. Think of the oxygen, the sun or water we cannot live without. God is good to people who do not even acknowledge Him. *"He makes His sun rise on the evil and on the good, and sends rain on the just and unjust" (Matthew 5:45 NKJV).*

Goodness is natural to God. It is like breathing. He does it all the time. To put it in poetic terms, *Goodness is God's heartbeat and His glory revealed.*

RECAP

- God is awesomely good. He is very rich in goodness.
- God is perfect, upright, kind, benevolent, wholesome, gracious and merciful.
- God declares things good when they are right and in perfect harmony with His character and intent.
- God does not just possess goodness or carry out good acts. Rather, He is GOODNESS, just like we know that God does not just love, but that He is LOVE.
- God is kind enough to spread His goodness our way, and not just keep it to Himself. God is not good just to some, but to all.
- This goodness we have in us has a source — God. After all, we are made in His image and likeness.
- In a world full of tragedies and injustices, God is still good, and will one day right the wrongs. Our job is to allow His goodness to flow through us to others.
- God is very predictable, meaning you can expect Him to be good all the time.
- God is good to people who do not even acknowledge Him. *"He makes His sun rise on the evil and on the good, and sends rain on the just and unjust" (Matthew 5:45 NKJV).*
- Goodness is quite natural to God. It is like breathing. He does it all the time. *Goodness is God's heartbeat and His glory revealed.*

=====================================

"When you put goodwill out there, it's amazing what can be accomplished."

Paul Walker

=====================================

Chapter 1: Freewill and Goodwill

The word "goodwill" — meaning, as its two parts suggest, engaging one's will in the execution of good deeds towards others — is used generously in the Bible. It refers to the showing of benevolence and charity that brings joy and warmth to many hearts. I particularly love the Christmas season. Every heart is turned towards doing extra good for others. It is a time of giving, rejoicing, reuniting and serving, as well as for joyous celebration. Carols are sung and love is expressed, and food is plenteous. It is a time when *Heaven kisses earth*. It is a wonderful reminder of God's goodness and love towards us.

It all started with God sending a Saviour to the world. No one coerced Him into doing this amazing act on our behalf. He exercised His freewill in an act of goodwill. The great joy of sending this precious gift would one day result in great pain for God when His only-begotten Son would hang on a cross — broken, bleeding and dying for humanity — yet God still did it, so we could rest assured that in His eyes we were well worth redeeming.

Jesus chose to forgive even while experiencing great suffering on the cross, as exemplified when He said this of the very people who were crucifying Him: *"Father, forgive them, for they do not know what they do" (Luke 23:34 NKJV)*. So many people go against God and His ways, thinking they are right. God is merciful and patient allowing them time to come to their senses and accept His truth. The nature of God is to forgive and redeem wicked, lost and broken humanity, not to abandon and destroy. The only thing He wants to destroy, in fact, is sin. Jesus died to destroy the works of Satan *(1 John 3:8)*.

If ever we doubt God's love and acceptance, just think back to this great act of goodwill: God sent Jesus into the world to be our Emmanuel (God with us). While the shepherds were minding their flocks in the field, angels appeared in bright light and told them about the good news that God was bringing the greatest gift to earth. *"For there is born to you this day in the city of David a Saviour, who is Christ the Lord. And this will be a sign to you: You will find a Babe wrapped in swaddling cloths, lying in a manger. And suddenly there was with the angel a multitude of heavenly host [many angels] praising God and saying: Glory to God in the highest, And on earth peace, goodwill toward men" (Luke 2:11–14 NKJV)*.

God exercised freewill in sending His Son to earth. He gave freewill to mankind, as well. I see it as one of the most powerful gifts God bestowed on us, beginning with Adam and Eve in the Garden of Eden. They had the ability to exercise choice, irrespective of other external or internal conditions. God Himself functions with freewill and His *will* is good. Everything He does is borne out of His own choosing, and whatever He does is always good, and God never does anything He does not want to.

Jesus came to earth to seek and save the lost because God willed it. That is a good choice. That good choice redeemed us and translated us into His Kingdom of light. Now, because we have freewill, God requires us to make a choice either to accept or to reject His gift. We are not robots. Adam and Eve were given a choice. God said they ought not to eat from the tree of the knowledge of good and evil *(Genesis 2:17)*. Satan tempted them in the hope that they would choose his lies and deception over God's truth, and they sided with him and lost their right standing with God. Notice, Satan could not make that choice for them. He cannot interfere with freewill.

Choices, borne out of freewill, have consequences. The results of their choice were overwhelmingly devastating. Death, sickness, war, poverty, injustices, murder, theft, lust and every other evil entered the earth and the lives of mankind through that door of disobedience. Freewill is great but also dangerous. We have to be responsible with it. God cannot be blamed for the failings of mankind. Those failings and tragedies are a result of choice.

God does not force anyone to accept Jesus as Saviour. God does not force people to love Him or serve Him. He does not even force people to be good. He allows each person to exercise freewill. If God took away freewill we would be reduced to the level of a programmed machine. We would not be held accountable for anything. God did not even force Jesus to die on the cross. Jesus chose to do that. It was what God the Father desired. But Jesus still had to choose it. Jesus said, *"I lay down my life that I may take it up again. No one takes it from me, but I lay it down of Myself. I have power to lay it down, and I have power to take it up again. This command I received from My Father"* (John 10:17–18 *NKJV*). I am glad He chose to align His will with the Father's.

Jesus struggled with the approaching cruel death He would face. In Gethsemane, He prayed, *"Abba Father, all things are possible for You. Take this cup away from Me; nevertheless, not what I will, but what You will"* (*Mark 14:36 NKJV*). The cup He wanted the Father to do away with was His crucifixion. Yet He bent His will to what the Father wanted. God the Father could have called off the crucifixion even at this point to spare His Son. Thank God, Jesus carried out the FATHER'S GOOD WILL. In Eden, Adam rejected God's good will and fell. In Gethsemane, Jesus accepted God the Father's good will and stood strong. By accepting and carrying out the Father's good will, Jesus procured victory for us over the Devil.

What are we doing with this powerful gift of freewill? Will we use it to do good things or carry out evil? Evil does not comprise just law-breaking and causes of emotional grievance, such as *murder, adultery or stealing*, but also offences such as *gossip, lying, pride, envy, jealousy* and *unbelief*. The list is long. We must examine our hearts daily so that these things do not take up residence in our lives. God has already punished Jesus for our sins. Why let them dominate our lives? He has given us power to overcome. Jesus defeated Satan, so we no longer have to remain under his bondage. That is why the Bible calls us overcomers *(1 John 5:4–5)*.

There is a call for us to do good to all, especially those who are the family of God *(Galatians 6:10)*. Even when people do not follow God, they will at least praise Him for the good acts they see us carry out. They will have no slanderous artillery to use against us, and should they make disreputable claims, these will be only rumours, for our integrity and good works will counteract any accusations. *"In all things showing yourself to be a pattern of good works; in doctrine showing integrity, reverence, incorruptibility, sound in speech that cannot be condemned; that one who is an opponent may be ashamed, having nothing evil to say of you"* (*Titus 2:7–8 NKJV*).

Many people are reaping the fruit of what they have sown. God cannot be blamed for that. God does not tempt mankind with sin *(James 1:13)*. He does not lead us into sin or darkness. People can blame Satan for those temptations, but that is about all. Even Satan cannot be blamed for their addictions. That is down to individual choice. *"But each one is tempted, when he is drawn away by his own desire and enticed"* (*James 1:14 NKJV*).

There are desires that are good. These are ones that do not violate God's Word. God blesses those desires that are pleasing to Him. Therefore, we ought to desire what is good. God said to His children, the Israelites, *"See, I have set before you life and death, blessing and cursing; therefore choose life, that both you and your descendants may live" (Deuteronomy 30:19 NKJV)*. God wants us to choose life and blessing, not things that bring pain and torment into our lives. Unfortunately, there are times when we suffer as a result of other people's bad choices or actions. They will be held accountable for that, not the innocent. God is a righteous judge. He is not in the business of letting the just suffer without justice.

Cain (Adam's firstborn son) had a choice to do good or evil to his brother Abel. He chose to do evil against his brother. God warned him that He must master the sin that was crouching in the shadows, ready to trap him in an act of evil. Cain, in his anger and jealousy, ignored God and killed Abel *(Genesis 4:7)*. Cain simply used his freewill to carry out evil. I am certain it must have pained God's heart when Cain did this. The evil Cain did came from the abuse of freewill. As aptly said by British novelist and theologian C. S. Lewis, *"Evil comes from the abuse of freewill."*

Parents normally expect their children to live a certain way under their care. As parents, they know more and generally have more wisdom. They endeavour to make wise choices for their children. There were times, growing up, when I thought I had more wisdom than my parents, only to land in trouble due to my so-called wise choices. As children mature, parents allow them to make their own choices, hoping they will apply the wisdom they received in their formative years. God expects us to make wise choices as we mature in His Kingdom.

After sin entered the earth, man still had that unique gift of freewill. It is hard to have two opposing voices constantly pulling us in different directions. There is the voice of God nudging us towards good and there is the deceptive voice of Satan we ought not to side with. We have the power to choose. Moses' successor, Joshua, challenged the people to make a choice as to whom they would serve: the true living God or the false gods of the Amorites. He then told them that he and his family chose to serve the true, living God *(Joshua 24:15–16)*. The people declared to Joshua that they would serve and obey the Lord. Then, in the hope that they would confirm their declaration with a corresponding action, he challenged them to get rid of their idols *(Joshua 24:23–24)*.

God does not take us from bondage to bondage, but rather, from bondage to freedom. The Israelites were not free to live as they desired under the cruel bondage of Egyptian slavery. God promised to free them so they could live without chains of oppression, and He alone can truly empower people to change and experience true freedom. This is freedom from fear, sin, insecurity, abuse, hopelessness and unhealthy addictions. God can provide a way out, but we have to take it, or stay trapped. Adhering to the principles of God ensures true freedom. Jesus said that if we accept and execute His truth we will be free indeed. *"Therefore if the Son [Word] makes you free, you shall be free indeed" (John 8:36 NKJV).*

God is good to us throughout our lives. His goodness is not seasonal. He does not change His mind regarding His goodness towards us. Anytime we are in need, God's goodness is available. He does not slumber, nor does He sleep *(Psalm 121:4–5)*. He is a 24/7 God. Here again, we see His freewill to do us good constantly, even when we have messed up. God does not base His goodness on our actions but on His character. If we dropped a thermometer into the pool of God's goodness, it will always read a hundred degrees or two hundred and twelve Fahrenheit.

Before we even realized we needed a Saviour, God had already decided to provide one. He made that decision without the counsel of a committee or board. He used His freewill for our goodwill. God desires something good to happen to us, not just through us. He will bring good to us as we release good to others. This creates a flow of goodness in our lives. That flow of goodness makes the world a better place. We must not choose things that pollute and block the flow of good. God's goodness is like water in the pipelines. It is always there. When we turn on the tap we will receive a flow. We must not stifle this flow of goodness.

When we work with God, we work for what is good. We cannot walk successfully with God unless we agree with Him. *Amos 3:3* says, *"Can two walk together unless they have agreed to do so?" (NIV)*. When we agree and walk in God's ways, we get God's results. We are encouraged to delight ourselves in the things of God, and He will give us the desires of our hearts *(Psalm 37:4)*. Before we could choose God, He first chose us *(John 15:16)*. God is constantly being gracious to us.

"But you are a chosen generation, a royal priesthood, a holy nation, His own special people, that you may proclaim the praises of Him who called you out of darkness into His marvellous light" (1 Peter 2:9 NKJV). We ought really to praise God, for all His choices bring blessing into our lives. God's choosing of us gives us a sense of value and acceptance. He has set us apart as His special people. He called us out of our mess and darkness, reformed us and placed us in His marvellous Kingdom of light. He made us part of His royal family.

Our physical birth was due to the will of our parents. But our spiritual rebirth is the will of God. *John 1:13* tells us that we are born again of the will of God, not the will of man. Without this rebirth we would never be close to God. We would never make it to Heaven. Thank God that He chose to regenerate us.

We can trust that whatever God does in us, it is for good, as is said in *Philippians 2:13: "For God who works in you both to will and to do for His good pleasure" (NKJV).* This allows us to trust Him and rest in Him even in the middle of a storm or trial in our lives, knowing that He is working for us a grand outcome. God orders the steps of a good man and delights in his way *(Psalm 37:23).* When a righteous man falls, God lifts him up *(Psalm 37:24).* We do not have to beg God for things He has already decided to do or provide for us. We must trust His timing. There is a time and season to all things. Waiting on God for something does not mean it is delayed. Rather, God knows the perfect time to release that blessing.

So what about the unrighteous? God's goodness allows Him to offer mercy and grace to them because God is not willing that any should perish *(2 Peter 3:9).* God's patience allows for repentance. Let us who are righteous in the Lord not forget that we were once alienated from Him, lost in our sin. He reached out and made us His family through reconciliation *(Romans 5:10).* Reconciliation is a ministry performed by God through the power of the Holy Spirit and the shed blood of Jesus. We received this reconcilement when we received Christ, signifying that reconciliation is a gift from God, the reconciler. The enmity or hostility between God and mankind was dealt with on the cross. Our once rebellious nature and dead spirit have been regenerated and reunited with God our Father, with whom we can enjoy communion and fellowship, having submitted to His Lordship.

It is not hard for God to choose good because He is good. He does not have to waver between blessing and cursing. Blessing is His first and only choice. The curse of sin and death came as a result of man's disobedience. It was not the will of God. God is a LIFE-GIVER. God is in the blessing business, not the cursing business. The curse of sin was dealt with on the cross. Adam's disobedience brought the curse, but Jesus' obedience brought blessing.

When God blesses, no curse can prosper. When Balaam was hired to curse the Israelites, he ended up pronouncing blessing. God did not listen to the wish of the Ammonites and Moabites to curse His people. Instead, He turned the curse into a blessing. *"The LORD your God would not listen to Balaam, but the LORD your God turned the curse into a blessing for you, because the LORD your God loves you"* (Deuteronomy 23:5 NKJV). God cannot be controlled or deceived. He does only what He chooses.

God is skilled at making good choices. This is enhanced by His omniscience. When God gives us knowledge, He wants us to use it in our decision-making. It is better to make choices with as much information and wisdom as possible. Even though God knows what the best choices are regarding our lives, He still lets us make our own. He trusts us with freewill. Therefore, we should be responsible with it.

RECAP

- God used His freewill in an act of goodwill when He sent Jesus to earth to die for humanity.
- While on the cross, Jesus used His will to forgive, rather than hold a grudge against humanity. While we were yet sinners Christ died for us.
- Jesus chose to use his freewill to destroy the works of Satan. But He chose to redeem mankind.
- God's goodness is seen in the life and light He brings to us. Satan is the thief and killer.
- In His goodness, God gave us the powerful gift of freewill.
- God desires we use our freewill for good.
- God delights in giving us the good desires of our hearts.
- The abuse of freewill leads to bondage and destruction.
- God's goodness lifts us up when we fall.
- God cannot be blamed for our wrong choices that bring us trouble instead of blessing.
- God is in the blessing business, not the cursing business.
- God is skilled at making good choices. This skill is enhanced by His omniscience.
- When God gives us knowledge and wisdom, He wants us to use them in our decision-making.

===================================

"Never lose an opportunity of seeing anything beautiful, for beauty is God's handwriting."

Ralph Waldo Emerson

===================================

Chapter 2: A Good Mouth and Good Hand

It is obvious from Scripture that God is a speaking God, and, like an artist uses his hands to create or paint a masterpiece, God is the ultimate master builder. He spoke creation into existence. Now that really sets Him apart as the one and only true God. In fact, He said, *"I am the first and I am the last; and beside Me there is no God. Indeed there is no other Rock [God]. I know not one" (Isaiah 44:6,8 NKJV).*

Some people seem surprised that God thinks and talks. Why would He give us mouths to speak and not have one for Himself? He speaks to us. He is a communicating God. He is not formless or speechless. God spoke to Moses face to face as one speaks to a friend *(Exodus 33:11).* God understands us and knows how to communicate with each of us in language and terms we understand best and to which we will be most receptive.

Given the fact that God speaks, we should be ready to listen. Being omniscient, God is able to reveal to us past, present and future things. God said, *"I will open My mouth in parables; I will utter things kept secret from the foundation of the world" (Matthew 13:35 NKJV).* God will tell us stories and in those stories will be revelations that impact our lives. In *Psalm 85:8,* David said, *"I will hear what God the LORD will speak: for He will speak peace to His people" (NKJV).* Would you not want God to speak, knowing that what He says is more profound than anything you can ever hope to hear?

God speaks in many ways. He uses words. He can speak through dreams and visions, and even through circumstances. He can put an idea or revelation in our hearts. God can use Scripture and other people to get a message to us. Whatever God has to say is very important. We would do well to listen and obey.

Unlike those of human beings, God's words have unlimited and sovereign power. God commands as King. We can hold on to every promise He has spoken to us in His Word. We are talking about a God who spoke light into existence *(Genesis 1).* We are talking about a God who called the dead out of graves; for example, Lazarus was dead for four days when Jesus called him out of the tomb and he emerged alive and well *(John 11:38–44).* The Word of God fixed everything that was dead and wrong in Lazarus, and God has life-giving words for whatever situation you are going through today.

In *Genesis 1*, God surveyed a dark and chaotic planet. I am glad He did not stay silent. I am also glad He did not say something like, *"Let it stay dark."* Rather, God opened His mouth and spoke wholesome and good things. He spoke words of life, order and beauty, all words that are reflective of His goodness.

He created a beautiful world, and then placed mankind in it. Of all He created, we are the crown of His handiwork. The next time you look in the mirror and admire yourself, remember God is the creator of such beauty. You have been beautifully and wonderfully created out of the goodness of God: *"I will praise You [Lord], for I am fearfully [amazingly] and wonderfully made; Marvellous are Your works; and my soul knows very well"* (Psalm 139:14 NKJV).

As much as God's creation is beautiful to behold, so is He. King David of Israel talked about beholding the beauty of the Lord *(Psalm 27:4)*. I believe when we see Jesus face-to-face , we are going to be in such awe of His beauty and goodness that we will be breathless. The apostle John gives us a wonderful glimpse of Jesus when the Holy Spirit opened his eyes to see into the realm of the supernatural: *"I turned around to see the voice that was speaking to me. And when I turned I saw seven golden lampstands, and among the lampstands was someone like the son of man [Jesus], dressed in a robe reaching down to his feet and with a golden sash around his chest. The hair on his head was white like wool, as white as snow, and his eyes were like blazing fire. His feet were like bronze glowing in a furnace, and his voice was like the sound of rushing waters … His face was like the sun shining in all its brilliance"* (Revelation 1:12–16, NIV). Furthermore, the angels and twenty-four elders in Heaven constantly worship and declare how awesome God is, as demonstrated when John of Patmos writes, *"You are worthy, O Lord, to receive glory and honour and power; for You created all things' and by Your will they exist and were created"* (Revelation 4:11 NKJV).

I was an art major student at university. Many times after working on an art project, I would stand back and be lost in wonder of what I had made. I was super-pleased that my art pieces were so good. I got the top award in both my second and third years. God did the same each time He fashioned something in the universe: He created it, then stood back and gloried in what excellence He had made. It was so good that He exclaimed, *"Oh, my, this is so good. I love it. I'm so pleased!"* Some people in their religious mindset just cannot picture God excited, giddy and skipping around with joy.

I believe one of the reasons why many people loved to be around Jesus was because He was fun and exciting.

Being a God of order and perfection, God beautified the planet: all the hills and valleys and oceans, the pretty flowers and towering trees. Think of all the beautiful sea and land creatures. Whenever I sit outside and watch a beautiful sunset, I cannot help but be in awe. God is a wonder, and He does wonderful things. The Bible says that not even Solomon was as beautifully arrayed as the flowers in the field that God had created *(Matthew 6:28–29)*. God is so good; no one can improve on His handiwork.

When God proclaimed that all He created was good, He was actually saying that it was perfect, pleasing and harmonious with Him. The chief manufacturer authenticated all of His creation as good. God has never created any substandard things. He does everything masterfully, because He is the Master.

God thought of everything when He fashioned us. Take a moment to reflect on your body, soul, and spirit, and you will realize how much detail and attention God put in when fashioning us. He was like a skilled potter working the clay *(Job 10:8)*. The physical body has the ability to regenerate cells and also heal itself. Every organ was intelligently designed to perform its unique function. Your digestive system works involuntary — you do not have to tell it to do its job. Your soul is so unique, enabling you to think, make sense of things and experience various emotions. Your spirit is eternal and God-breathed. It is the real you that God placed in your physical body. Your spirit has the ability to communicate with God.

Our God speaks good things and does good things. God is not willing to stay silent. He speaks life and healing into our lives. When Jesus encountered the sick, He touched them and spoke words of healing and they recovered. Jesus met a man with a crippled hand. Jesus commanded him to stretch out his hand. From that moment the man's crippled hand was completely restored *(Mark 3:3–5)*. The centurion captain asked Jesus to speak a word of healing over one of his servants who was very sick. Jesus spoke a word of healing and that centurion's servant was healed *(Luke 7:3–10)*.

We do not have a lack of God's Word in our modern day. We have no excuse concerning the Word of God. He speaks mainly through His Word. When people and nations reject God's Word, they are rejecting His voice. Without His voice, we will lose our way. Indeed, even in our prayer lives, God wants us to speak His Word and get His results. God does not speak condemnation over us *(Romans 8:1)*. Parents speak blessing over their children because they love them and desire a good outcome for them, and because they know the power of their words. God does the very same thing to us. His words have greater power. He uses those words to speak blessing over us.

When God's Word is rejected, then His goodness gets rejected too. Many people want the good things God provides, but fail to seek His face. God is not just about principle, but also about personhood. God wants to be personal with us. He is relational, not just structural and constitutional. God regenerated our spirits and placed His Holy Spirit in us so we can be in fellowship with Him. He wants to talk to us and love us. God makes us His primary business.

There is a level of wisdom that comes only from God. Man's wisdom is limited. The Bible declares that God's wisdom is higher than the wisdom of man. When we reject God's Word, we are actually rejecting His wisdom. *Jeremiah 8:9* says, *"The wise men are ashamed, They are dismayed and taken. Behold, they have rejected the word of the LORD; So what wisdom do they have?" (NKJV)*. Let me say this: if man's wisdom goes against God's Word, then man's wisdom is foolishness. Many times, people pierce themselves with all kinds of troubles for a lack of godly wisdom. Instead of blaming others, God or the circumstance, apply godly wisdom to right the mess. Experience God's best by applying God's wisdom. God's wisdom guarantees success. God told Abraham to circumcise his son when he turned eight days old. God had all the knowledge and wisdom to know that the eighth day was the best day for circumcision for a baby, because vitamin K (which enables blood to coagulate) is fully present on day eight. Also, prothrombin (necessary for the blood-clotting process) is 110% on day eight. Abraham did not have the wisdom to know this back then. But he obeyed God and got the best results. If he had circumcised the baby on day one, he would have risked severe bleeding. In our modern day hospitals give babies a vitamin K shot to safeguard against this. There were no hospitals to present Abraham's son with a vitamin K shot back then.

Whenever God speaks, we can be certain that wisdom is present. We must value the words from God's mouth. He speaks them to make us wise. The Bible encourages us to get wisdom, for it is very important. It is the principal thing. It is to be prioritized *(Proverbs 4:7).* If there is a philosophy that seems transcendent but contradicts or violates the Bible, we are far better off dropping that philosophy and sticking with God's Word. God's Word will bless us through this life and take us beyond the grave. Man's words and philosophies cannot take us beyond the grave. They die right there.

God is so good, He cannot lie or fail. We will never find evil, malice or confusion on His lips. God speaks only righteousness. Whatever He says, He does. There is direct correlation between His mouth and hand. To reiterate, God speaks truth *(Numbers 23:19).* Bitter and sweet water cannot flow from the same fountain. We should not use our mouths to bless God while cursing others *(James 3:9–12).* God wants us to bless, not curse. Continual verbalization of bitterness and cursing is evidence of a bitter and cold heart *(Hebrews 12:15).* That is where the change is needed, for the mouth speaks only that which is in the heart. God speaks life, blessing and hope because He is full of these.

Why speak death when God is busy speaking life? Many people ignorantly speak death and hopelessness over themselves, not understanding the power of the tongue. Rather, they ought to use their mouths as a fountain of life. Do not become a broken fountain and a corrupt spring. We must be springs that bring out fresh, life-giving water over ourselves and others instead of murky and stale words of bondage.

Being a word-based species, we readily use words as a primary form of communication. We need to examine our words before speaking. Impulsive words that are negative and crushing can hurt or offend others. When those words or that tweet is out, it is hard to retract them. Words hurt just as much as a physical beating. The tongue is a small member of the body, yet it can do much good or bad *(James 3:6).* Gossip and false rumours can destroy relationships *(Proverbs 20:19).* Our Christian witness becomes useless when we contradict it with our tongues. The Bible says, *"If anyone among you thinks he is religious, and does not bridle [discipline] his tongue but deceives his own heart, this one's religion is useless" (James 1:26 NKJV).* We ought to be above reproach in word and in action.

Many people want God to continue speaking and doing good while they continue speaking corruption and doing evil. They seem to forget that God is interested in changing their speaking and behaviour to line up with His. We get God's results when we align ourselves with Him. People who oppose God in speech and deed hardly benefit from His wisdom. *Proverbs 3:7* admonishes us to lean on God and access His wisdom, not our own foolish ways.

God has a good hand. Ezra had made a long journey from Babylon to Jerusalem safely and successfully because God watched over him, protected him and favoured him *(Ezra 7:9)*. That phrase *good hand* is a symbol of God's power. It signifies that God uses His power to bless and help us. When God's good hand is upon us, good things happen, despite the troubles in this world, or the persecution that the enemy brings our way. God puts His powerful hand upon us to do us good. God's hand also represents his provision. *Psalm 104:28* says, *"When You open Your hand, they are satisfied with good things" (NIV).* The birds do not plant and harvest, yet they are well fed. God makes sure that they are. We can expect God to meet our needs, seeing as we are far more valuable than birds.

God used His own hand (power) and worked salvation and restoration for us. No one else could save us but God. Using His power exclusively for good, He is in the business of destroying evil, but salvaging sinners, on the condition that they choose to accept His redemptive plan. As I have mentioned before, God is patient, not willing that any should perish, but rather come to repentance *(2 Peter 3:9)*.

God understands beauty and attractiveness, symmetry and pleasantness, and He knows exactly how to make something look its best and work at its optimum. He takes broken lives and masterfully reforms them into glorious testimonies of His goodness. He is an artist with a very skilled hand. He fashioned Adam and Eve beautifully. He created them perfect in body, soul and spirit. They were as holy and righteous as God Himself. There was nothing missing or broken in their make-up. Our holy and righteous God cannot create unholy and flawed things. God is an artist who pays careful attention to even the minutest detail. I am always in awe of God's genius when I look at His creation. *Psalm 8:4–6* says, *"What is man that You [God] are mindful of him?... You have crowned him with glory and honour. You have made him to have dominion over the works of Your hands; You have put all things under his feet" (NKJV).*

God invested so much in us. *Ephesians 2:10* tells us that we are God's handiwork, created in Christ Jesus to do good works, which God prepared in advance. God determined our make-up, gifts and abilities. God determined our purpose. He destined us for greatness, not a mediocre existence In *Jeremiah 29:11*, God says, *"I know the thoughts I think towards you" (NKJV)*. In other words, God is aware of what He has in mind concerning our lives. He plans our lives purposefully. None of us is an afterthought. God then goes on to tell us what kind of thoughts He has concerning us. *"Thoughts of peace and not evil" (NKJV)*. This is reassuring, to know that God seeks to do us good and bring us hope, and have us live confidently with great expectation, and not in fear and uncertainty. He then goes on to say, *"to give you an expected end" (NKJV)*. God wants us to know that our future is secure in Him. We will not end in disaster but in victory and triumph.

God is mindful of us. We are not just a statistic to Him. No one is a mistake, even if our birth was a surprise to our parents. God knew we were coming to earth. He was already prepared for us. The Bible declares that God has written our names on the palm of His hand. *Isaiah 49:16* says, *"See, I have inscribed you on the palms of My hands; Your walls [life] is continually before Me" (NKJV)*. This speaks of closeness, love and care. God is always aware of us. God gives sun and rain for our good. Yet there is probably nothing greater than the Son He sent to us to shine light on our darkened souls. Jesus the Son did the hard thing by dying for us so we could be free and live in comfort and assurance of a bright future. He gave us the precious Holy Spirit, guaranteeing our Heavenly inheritance.

Nothing is too hard for God. The Bible declares that all things are possible with God *(Matthew 19:26)*. God asked Moses a question while he was tasked with leading about two million Israelites to the Promised Land: *"Has the LORD's arm been shortened?"* (Numbers 11:23 *NKJV)*. In other words, *"Do you think I have reached my limit? Do you think my power is insufficient? Do you think I have ever encountered a problem I have not already provided an answer for?"*

This question was posed to Moses because he could not see how God would provide food for so many people in the desert. To paraphrase, Moses, annoyed and overwhelmed, says to God, *"There are so many people here. Shall all the herds and flock of cattle we have be slaughtered to feed them? Are you going to send us fish from the sea, seeing as we are in the middle of a desert? How is it even possible to satisfy so many people in the middle of nowhere" (Numbers 11:21–22).* Nothing catches God by surprise. The Bible says that God already knows what we need even before we ask. He may not do it the way we expect, but He will definitely do it.

Reading through the Bible, I have come to the conclusion that nothing amazes or alarms God more than unbelief. God wants to be believed. Jesus marvelled when people displayed great faith in God and His power and goodness. Yet He also marvelled at some people's unbelief. Jesus took issue with the Pharisees for their lack of belief in Him as the Messiah and often harshly rebuked them *(Matthew 16:1–6)*. He praised those who trusted in Him as Saviour, healer and provider.

A Gentile woman besought Jesus to heal her daughter who was vexed by a demonic spirit. We understand that, during His earthly ministry, Jesus was sent only to the Jewish people first. He told her He was sent to the Jews, but because she persisted and would not give up, He healed her daughter after commending her faith. Jesus said, *"O woman, great is your faith! Let it be to you as you desire. And her daughter was healed from that very hour" (Matthew 15:28 NKJV).*

Many years ago, in my teen years, I would frequently help my mother with the daily washing. I was always amazed at how clean her washing was. People passing by the house would marvel at her brilliantly clean clothes, given the fact that she did not possess a washing machine. Everything was hand-washed, even the sheets and blankets. Every clothing item would go through a thorough wash and then through two and sometimes three rinses. After a final examination, they would be hung on the line. Those precious hands of my mother were responsible for the washing of fourteen family members, week in and week out. She did it without complaint or resentment. I learned some valuable lessons from her. She did everything with excellence, whether cleaning, cooking, shopping or washing clothes. Similarly, God does things with excellence and expects us to do likewise. *Ecclesiastes 9:10* says, *"Whatever your hand finds to do, do it with your might" (NKJV).* Even when people fail to recognise or reward our good work, we continue to do it as unto the Lord. God gives us strength to do good works. Our works are established by His power *(Psalm 90:17).*

The world needs our good works. If we fold our hands and our good works weaken, evil will flourish even more. We are God's vessels. He uses us to do His good bidding in the earth. Personally, I do not want to be a vessel stranded in the clutches of mediocrity and indifference. Rather, I want to be a vessel strong and available for the master's use. If there is something good and impactful that I can do, then I ought to do it, instead of waiting or hoping someone else will step in. We ought to be passionate and channel that passion into action.

It is quite tragic when so-called people of God use their hands to carry out wrong instead of good. The wicked are known for acts of evil, but ambassadors of goodness ought to be known for good acts. *Jeremiah 23: 14* says, *"Also I have seen a horrible thing in the prophets of Jerusalem: They commit adultery and walk in lies; They also strengthen the hands of the evildoers" (NKJV).* Justice fails when those in power fail to uphold the law and administer justice, and when they themselves are guilty of acts of injustice. They are only furthering the cause of the wicked, leaving them to go unpunished. Accountability does matter. *James 4:8* calls for us to have clean hands and purified hearts. This is about cleaning the inside rather than just the outside. It is pointless to look good externally but internally be broken and depraved.

The Bible says that the heart of the king is in the hand of God *(Proverbs 21:1)*. In other words, God can change the heart and mind of rulers to accomplish His purposes. This is evident time and time again throughout history. There are many true stories of people who were instantly transformed by God while carrying out acts of evil: for example, King Darius ended up changing a decree that excluded God to include Him as the One and only true, powerful God throughout his kingdom after God delivered Daniel from the lions *(Daniel 6:4–28)*; Saul (the persecutor of the early church believers) was converted to Christianity while persecuting Christians; and Balaam (a prophet who used his gift for selfish gain and evil) ended up blessing the Israelites while attempting to curse them.

The hands of Jesus are symbolic of good works. He created a beautiful planet for our habitation. He touched the sick and they were healed. He broke bread and fed multitudes. These same hands were nailed to a cross where He made the ultimate sacrifice for our redemption. When Thomas doubted that Jesus had risen from the dead, Jesus invited Thomas to reach out and touch His hands and side. This was evidence of the nail-pierced hands and pierced side of the Messiah *(John 20:27)*. These were the hands of our Saviour. These were good hands that did a good work. Jesus put His hands to a good cause. He wants us to do the same. It is tragic to put one's hands to a task that ultimately yields sorrow or pain instead of good. Many times people blame God for the pain they have caused themselves. God uses His hands to build us, not destroy us. What are we using our hands for?

Many times, God rescued Israel out of the hand or hold of other nations who came against them. God delivered them because His hand is stronger than that of the enemy. When God called Gideon, he was hiding in a wine press, threshing wheat, for the Midianites used to raid the crops of the Israelites at harvest time. God empowered Gideon to defeat the Midianites who had brought fear and frustration to them. *Judges 6:14* says, *"And the LORD turned to him [Gideon] and said, 'Go in this might of yours, and you shall save Israel from the hand of the Midianites. Have I not sent you?'" (NKJV)*.

We must stay the course with God. He is doing a great handiwork in our lives. It may not seem like it at the start or middle of the process, but rest assured, He will make it all good in the end. God's hand is for us, not against us. Being under His right hand is about being in a place of honour and favour. Great things happened with the early church. Many were getting saved and many great miracles were taking place. This was all happening because the Lord's hand was with them *(Acts 11:21)*. In our day and age we are commissioned to do great things because God's hand is still working on our behalf. When God's hand is on our side, we have access to His power, favour, grace and provisions. We have nothing to fear. Children do not fear when they are held in the strong arms of their parents. God holds us close. We are safe in the Father's arms.

RECAP

- God is a speaking God, and like an artist would use his hands to create or paint a masterpiece, God is the ultimate master builder.
- God understands us and He knows how to communicate with us.
- Given the fact that God speaks, we should be ready to listen. Being omniscient, God is able to reveal to us past, present and future things.
- God is so good; no one can improve on his handiwork.
- When people and nations reject God's Word, they are rejecting His voice. Without His voice (direction), we will lose our way.
- God's Word will bless us through this life and take us beyond the grave. Man's words and philosophies cannot take us beyond the grave. They die right there.
- Our Christian witness becomes useless when we contradict it with our tongues and actions.
- When God's good hand is upon us, good things happen, despite the troubles in this world, or the persecution the enemy brings our way.
- God understands and knows exactly how to make something look its best and work at its optimum. He is an artist with very skilled hands.
- The world needs our good works. If we fold our hands and our good works weaken, evil will flourish even more.

==

"In God's eyes, love is never absent. In God's heart, forgiveness is never impossible. In God's embrace, no one is ever alone or forgotten."

Azgraybebly Josland

==

Chapter 3: Father Heart of God

"Good, Good Father" is the title of a song our worship band sings at church. It is the absolute truth — God is a good Father!

I spent three months at Addington Hospital on the east coast of Durban city in South Africa. A major burn on my right shoulder and upper arm landed me there. As a five-year-old, being in hospital as a result of suffering a physical trauma was a terrifying experience, not to mention the added anxiety of being away from my family. I briskly came to appreciate the simple pleasures of home: I missed playing with my siblings, my mother's fine cooking and the songs she would hum while busily tending to the household chores, the smell of our dirt yard, and being in the arms of my father and mother, as well as my grandmother.

Day after day, I looked forward to the visits from my parents and uncle, but it was my father who visited me more often than the others. I hated it when he said goodbye, and I would console myself in the knowledge that one day I would be going home, where I desired to be. We long for God our Father because He feels like home. His presence is our safe place. It is our place of contentment.

The day the hospital declared me fit to return home was exciting for me. I could not wait for my father to get me out of there. Do not get me wrong, the nurses and doctors were great. The hospital food and desserts were fine, and their beds were pretty soft and comfortable, better than the floor I slept on at home. Yet home was home, no matter how great or small some of its comforts were. Home was the best place to be.

Finally, the day came when my father fetched me from the hospital. By the time we got off the bus in our home town, it was quite dark. We had to walk along a path between houses to get to our house on Thornwood Road. I remember a dog rushing towards us with a menacing bark. I cried out in fear. My father immediately scooped me up into his arms and said two words that drove that fear away and calmed me down: *"I'm here."*

I knew he would protect me with his life. He would not allow that dog to harm me. He would defend me completely. Right then and there my father's arms were my safe place, my comfort and my advantage point. I needed someone stronger, wiser and bigger than myself. My father was that man. There were many other times in my youth when he stood in the gap for me and my siblings. My father was always going to be there for us and care for us. It was one of the most reassuring things. No matter how much trouble our family faced, my father never left, and neither did my mother. They were committed to us, oftentimes facing various discomforts themselves to allow us some comforts.

We believed in our father and we trusted him. Yes, I guess I am bragging about my father. But let me switch over and begin to brag about another Father I have. He is God, my Heavenly Father; and He is yours, too, if you have made Jesus the Saviour and Lord of your life *(John 1:12)*. God is family-orientated. He does not believe in religion, neither did it originate with Him. Family originated with Him. In the Gospels we get to see how close Jesus was to the Father, an apt example for us to follow. Jesus was one with the Father *(John 1:18)*. Jesus knew the Father's heart, the Father's voice and the Father's desires.

God the Father is the One who gave me my earthly father, allowing him to model the father's heart of God. Even though my earthly father was not perfect, I saw these wonderful paternal characteristics in him. Even though my earthly father eventually grew sick and died, God was never going to expire. He is still with me. The wonderful reality is that I will get to see my earthly father again in Heaven, thanks to the goodness of my Heavenly Father. He made this possible through the crucifixion of His Son.

God is our loving Father who loves with the heart of a Father. Someone once wrote, *"God cannot stop loving."* This is so true. Every human being who ever existed was created by God. But to become God's child, a person has to be born again. Our very first earthly father Adam disobeyed and plunged all mankind into sin *(Genesis 3)*. We were all born with this fallen, sinful nature in us. It is called the Adamic nature. God requires that we be born again to become His legitimate children. To reiterate, *John 1: 12* says, *"as many as received Him [Jesus], to them He gave the right to become children of God, to those who believe in His name"* (NKJV).

God our Father does not want us out but in. For instance, in the beginning, God, being a loving and righteous Father, placed Adam and Eve in a perfect environment with all they needed. Much to their immediate regret, they opened the door to sin by choosing Satan's suggestion and deception over God's good commands. As a consequence, in *Genesis 3:22–24*, God expelled Adam and Eve from the Garden of Eden, not out of coldness or a bankruptcy of sympathy, but because God did not want them to reach out and eat from the tree of life and live forever in a state of unrighteousness or fallen nature. With the Fall came evil of all kinds, and the things that are adverse to mankind were empowered through sin. Sickness, death, worry, aging and murder were some of the things sin empowered.

Since sin imprisons us so desperately, Father God commands us to do not evil but good. His commands are holy, just and good *(Romans 7:12)*. He will never hold His creation hostage. He longs to lead us from bondage to freedom; from darkness to light. Because God's commands are so good, King David said, *"Your commands are my delight" (Psalm 119:143 NKJV)*. Whatever God commanded David to do brought peace, joy and prosperity to his life. The only persecution he faced was from those who were jealous and intimidated by his God-given success, and his own self-inflicted sorrows as a result of his sinful acts.

Not all people delight in God's commands. We see this played out all over the world. People always question or go against what God wills. They then encounter adversity and God gets the blame. The Bible says that if you suffer or are punished for doing evil, you deserve it. Then it also says that if you suffer for righteousness' sake, you will be commended and rewarded. Paul and Silas were beaten and thrown in prison just for doing good, which was preaching the Gospel. They were doing God's work. They were suffering for righteousness' sake. God delivered them from prison and continued to bless their lives. On the other hand, if someone is thrown into prison for committing a crime or some punishable act, then they have no one to blame but themselves.

God, being a good Father, had a plan of salvation to redeem people from Satan's kingdom of darkness and place them in His Kingdom of light. This is why the Bible says that Jesus, the Son of God, was prepared before the foundations of the world to be the sacrificial lamb to die for our sins. The sacrificial lamb symbolized the innocent dying for the guilty. *1 Peter 1:18–19* says, *"For you know that God paid a ransom to save you from the empty life you inherited from your ancestors. And it was not paid with mere gold or silver, which lose their value. It was the precious blood of Christ, the sinless, spotless Lamb of God" (NLT).*

Jesus laid down His life willingly. In *John 10:11*, He told us He is the good shepherd who gave His life for His sheep (mankind). God took His dear and beloved Son and allowed Him to be crucified so we would not perish in Hell. He did it so we would become His legitimate children. That is the greatest act of love. *"For God so loved the world that He gave His only begotten Son, that whoever believes in Him should not perish but have everlasting life" (John 3:16 NKJV).* When we are tempted to doubt God's love and goodness, just think on this great act of love.

God is just and fair. He cannot tolerate or turn a blind eye to sin. He Himself said that the soul that sins shall die. But He also made provision for eternal life through Jesus Christ's blood sacrifice on the cross: *"The wages of sin is death; but the gift of God is eternal life in Christ Jesus our Lord" (Romans 6:23 NKJV).* The final reward or result of sin is death and destruction, whereas the reward or payment of accepting Jesus as a gift is eternal life. There is Hell to gain for sin, but Heaven to gain for accepting righteousness through Christ.

DIVINE PROVIDER

The nature of a father is to provide for his offspring. He tends to their needs and wants. He shelters them, feeds them, educates them, protects them and guides them. He offers love and affection. This itemisation of characteristics operates as a reflection of our Heavenly Father. David said that he would not want or be in need because God was His shepherd *(Psalm 23:1)*. He realized that God is a good Father who will tend to the needs of His children.

People who doubt God's goodness and His willingness to bless ought to read what Jesus said about God the Father. In *Matthew 7*, Jesus encourages us to ask of God for that which we need. If God was not in the business of providing, Jesus would not have told us to ask. *"Ask, and it will be given to you; seek, and you will find; knock, and it will be opened to you" (Matthew 7:7 NKJV).* He went on to say that those who ask do receive, and for those who knock, the door shall be opened to them, and those who seek, do find. God did say that we will find Him when we seek for Him *(Jeremiah 29:13)*.

Jesus pointed out that if a sinful earthly father knows how to give good gifts to his children, how much more our Heavenly Father who is perfect *(Matthew 7:11)*. God is a giver of all that is wholesomely good. *"Every good gift and every perfect gift is from above, and comes down from the Father of lights, with whom there is no variation or shadow of turning" (James 1:17 NKJV)*. God's gifts are not broken and they are not harmful. When we ask Him for things, we can expect the best.

FATHERS PROVIDE LOVE

Children thrive when they receive a good daily dose of fatherly love. A father will always be a father. Even when children have grown up, fathers still matter. When my father died several years ago, I suddenly knew what it felt like to have my strong pillar and rock gone. I felt this void. Thank God He knows how to comfort us in our times of great need.

When I was young and unmarried, I always wondered what it would feel like to be a father. After fifteen years of fatherhood and two boys, I can say it is a sacred, joyous and special role. It is also a daunting and challenging one. Our children are depending on us parents to meet their daily needs. They crave our time, affection and attention in pretty large doses. Fatherhood is more than just impregnating a woman. That is just the start.

After the birth of my first son, it all being new to me, I cried. It was a mixture of joy, awe and uncertainty. Was I ready for this? I was now responsible for a new life, a gift from God. I had a deep and almost unexplainable love for this newborn. Similarly, this happened again when my second son was born.

Children and adults do not do too well emotionally and psychologically when love is absent from their lives. Before God sent Jesus to die for us, He told us that He loved us. He understands that we need love. As an earthly father, everything I do for my boys is filtered through love. That love causes me to do everything for their benefit. Love makes the sacrifices worthwhile.

The Father is motivated by love. His love is not seasonal or conditional. He loves us all the time. *"The LORD has appeared of old to me, saying: 'Yes, I have loved you with an everlasting love; Therefore with lovingkindness I have drawn you'" (Jeremiah 31:3 NKJV)*. God's love drives away fear and insecurities. His love is so perfect, fear cannot operate around it. *"There is no fear in love; but perfect love casts out fear" (1 John 4:18 NKJV).* When a father is harsh and violent towards his child, that child will experience fear and insecurity. Yet, when a father acts kindly and lovingly towards a child, that child experiences love and security and feels safe.

Jesus admonished His disciples to love one another genuinely. This love bond would be a sign to the world that they were His disciples *(John 13:34–35).* Jesus did not say healing, power or prosperity would be that sign, but love. Out of love flows healing, power, wealth and restoration.

FATHERS PROVIDE COVERING

Fathers are the head. They are the director in the family production. They carry vision and direction for the family. They supervise and provide oversight. They look at the big picture. They work to cover the family's needs. They provide a safe haven for the family members. When in dire situations, the family members look to their covering for consolation and direction. I love that line in that song that says: *"I go to the rock that is higher than I."* This song points mankind to God, the ultimate Father.

When God finally brought Israel out of Egypt, He decided not to lead them through the land of the Philistines, because their hearts were not ready for war in the likely case it broke out. God knew better and his leading proved it *(Exodus 13:17).* Therefore, God led them through the desert another way. As a Father, God leads us in paths of righteousness. Children may not always fully understand the leading of their fathers, but rest assured, they have checked out the paths ahead and have decided on the best ones for their children's sake.

God, as Father, is our ultimate covering. He provides a place for us. It is called His Kingdom. Every house needs a roof; otherwise its contents are left to the mercy of the elements. The roof protects all that is under it. When we come under God, we receive His divine covering, which offers security and comfort. Sometimes we do not even realize how many bad things God shields us from daily. *"He shall cover you with His feathers, And under His wings you shall take refuge; His truth shall be your shield and buckler. You shall not be afraid of the terror by night, Nor of the arrow that flies by day, Nor the pestilence that walks in darkness, Nor of the destruction that lays waste at noonday" (Psalm 91:4–6 NKJV).*

FATHERS PROVIDE PROTECTION

Fathers provide protection from various kinds of harm and danger. They have to protect their families from physical harm and other abuses, whether sexual, verbal, emotional or social. How many stories do we hear of teenagers committing suicide just from cyber bulling? Like God our Father actively watches over us and protects us, and builds us up and restores us, so too must fathers be watchful. Fathers must make it a habit to familiarise themselves with today's technology and social media aptly to know and guide their children, and protect them from the pitfalls and dangers that surround them. Know who your children are friends with. Help them choose healthy friendships. Teach them about their self-worth and respect. Teach them how to make wise choices. Teach them how to avoid being abused by others, whether physically, emotionally, sexually or psychologically. The generation of children today are drawn to social media. They are drawn to movies, fashion, tech devices and celebrities. They get bombarded by so much on social media. It is almost unavoidable. Fathers must teach them to be smart and savvy with regard to their devices and social media.

Before David became king, he was a shepherd boy. He was tasked with minding the sheep. The sheep belonged to his father Jesse. David had to find green pasture for them and guard them from enemies. He would endanger his life against the lion and the bear just to protect the sheep, slaying both ferocious beasts *(1 Samuel 17:34–36)*. A hired hand would have probably run off, leaving the sheep in danger of being torn apart by these ferocious enemies. But not David. He was brave, confident in his God, and a true and faithful shepherd of his father's flock. As fathers, we care for children who are actually God's. As stewards of such awesome gifts, we have to do our best to nurture and protect them. We take ownership and responsibility over what God has entrusted to us.

Jesus called Himself the good shepherd who laid down His life for the sheep, just like David was willing to do day after day. God never abandons His sheep. Even though we cannot see them, we have assurance in *Psalm 91:11* that God has provided angelic beings at our side: *"For He shall give His angels charge over you, To keep you in all your ways" (NKJV)*.

FATHERS PROVIDE DISCIPLINE

Love disciplines. God our Father loves — and so, disciplines us. If we refuse or reject God's discipline we are practically saying He is not our Father. It is the Father's nature to watch over us, correct us and steer us into safety. *Proverbs 3:11–12* says, *"My son, do not despise the chastening of the LORD, Nor detest His correction; For whom the LORD loves He corrects, Just as a father the son in whom he delights" (NKJV)*.

God is the kind of Father who will not allow us to go uncorrected (undisciplined), and neither will he permit the wrong thing to destroy us. However He will not violate our choice. When our children do wrong we, as parents, correct them, knowing full well that we will have to correct them many times over in the future because they will do more wrong as a result of freewill and a flawed nature. After Adam and Eve chose to disobey, God still showed up. He showed up to deal with the situation. The concern God shows is because He cares so much: hence, it is in His nature to reprimand but also apply grace.

God confronted His children in the Garden and meted out punishment for their wrong *(Genesis 3:16–17)*. However, He also provided a way out when He started the redemption process *"Also for Adam and his wife the LORD God made tunics of skin, and clothed them" (Genesis 3:21 NKJV)*. It must have broken His heart when His children chose the evil words of Satan over His good and life-giving words. There is nothing good that comes from Satan. He seeks only to deceive, to steal, to cause pain and to kill. He deceived Eve, and still seeks to deceive many today.

We see in *Genesis 6* God looking down upon the earth and, seeing that the wickedness of man had filled the earth, God was sorry that He had created mankind. Man's wickedness grieved His heart *(Genesis 6:5–6)*. Growing up, there were things that my siblings and I did that hurt or angered our parents. Their reaction was purely out of love and concern. They expected better. They gave us the very best they could offer. The least we could have done was honour them.

Discipline can conjure up all kinds of feelings depending on how it is viewed or the experience one endured. Abuse is not discipline. If the discipline is causing serious injury, whether physical or emotional, then it is unhealthy. Discipline in God's view is not to destroy but correct and redirect. People who constantly reject discipline hardly end up at the destinations they desired. Many years ago one of my pastoral leaders at a church school I worked at disciplined me over an issue that was bringing reproach to the school and to me. The choice was simple. They would work with me and pray with me to help bring correction and change. I had the choice of humbling myself and accepting the discipline and help or walking away in arrogance. I chose to get help and change. I remember the wise advice this particular leader gave me, and it has stayed with me for many years. I have used his wise words to steer my life in the right direction. He said, *"Aubrey, you are very gifted and popular, and that is great. But some aspects of your character are letting you down. You cannot have a balanced and successful life by only focusing on your gifts and ignoring your character. Develop your character and it will keep you in the positions your talents and gifts take you into."*

This brings to mind the care a shepherd has for his sheep. He uses his rod to drive away the enemy, but uses his staff gently to lead and guide the sheep *(Psalm 23:4)*. God uses His Word and the Holy Spirit to lead and guide us. Through His Word, we are admonished and ought to change as the Word directs. If we do not heed God's disciplinary measures, then adverse circumstances end up forcing us to surrender to His way. People who continually reject God's discipline are only hurting themselves.

FATHERS PROVIDE SUSTENANCE

Every family needs sustenance. A new-born baby depends on its mother for food in the form of milk. Children are helpless and need parents to provide their food and other materials to exist. They need clothes, shoes, shelter, books, toys, transport and so on. In other words, they need to be sustained, and someone must have the resources to provide that sustenance. *1 Timothy 5:8* tells us that a father who neglects the needs of his family is worse than an infidel (unbeliever).

Therefore, God empowers fathers with skills and abilities to acquire those resources to sustain their families. We see this even with many animals that sustain their young, up until a point when they can take care of themselves. Worry comes from not knowing where our sustenance will come from. But, when we do know, we quit being fretful or anxious. Knowing the Lord was his true sustainer, King David said, *"I lay down and slept; I woke, for the LORD sustained me"* *(Psalm 3:5 NKJV)*. Father God does not want us to live in anxiety but in rest and confidence in His ability to meet our needs. In the third Psalm, David says that he enjoys peaceful sleep, knowing that when he wakes, God is there to meet his needs. In light of this incredible truth, why should he worry about anything?

When the Israelites were journeying through the desert, God sustained them with manna and quail for food *(Exodus 16)*. He even brought water out of a dry rock to quench their thirst *(Exodus 17)*. In the day He would provide cloud cover over them against the harsh desert sun. At night, He provided a pillar of fire to keep them warm. He was mindful of what they needed.

FATHERS BLESS

The blessing of the father is important. The things we say to our children are important. They matter. As fathers, we ought to speak life-giving words over them. God did not give us children to curse or hurl verbal abuse and insults at. Negative words and actions affect the confidence and outlook of children.

The blessing of the father does not have to be only for special occasions. Fathers can speak blessings over their children daily. When fathers bless they are empowering their children and also strengthening their relationship with them. They are affecting their future. Some children do not even know what the blessing of the father looks like, sounds like or feels like. Not everyone in the world will speak positively over our children. That is why we must make their home experience a place of affirmation and approval. The Bible is filled with accounts of aging fathers laying hands and bestowing blessings on their children. Speak health, protection and well-being over your children.

Jacob (the grandson of the Old Testament patriarch Abraham) sought his father's blessing. He deceived his father Isaac into giving him the blessing of the firstborn even though he was not the firstborn son *(Genesis 27:5–29)*. His older twin brother Esau was very distraught when he found out that his father had been tricked into bestowing the blessing meant for him on his younger brother, Jacob. Nevertheless, we see how much these sons valued the father's blessing. There was power in the blessing. Let me quote the blessing Isaac had reserved for his firstborn son:

"Surely the smell of my son is like the smell of a field which the LORD has blessed. Therefore may God give you of the dew of heaven, of the fatness of the earth, and plenty of grain and wine. Let peoples serve you, and nations bow down to you. Be master over your brethren, and let your mother's sons bow down to you. Cursed be everyone who curses you, and blessed be those who bless you" (Genesis 27:27–29 NKJV).

Grandfathers can also speak blessings over their grandchildren. Jacob (Israel) laid his hands on his grandsons, Manasseh and Ephraim, and blessed them *(Genesis 48:17–21)*. God started the whole blessing thing by speaking blessing over Adam and Eve after He created them. Let us continue blessing our children.

RECAP

- We long for God our Father because He feels like home. His presence is our safe place.
- My father was there for us and cared for us. It was one of the most reassuring things.
- Every human being who ever existed was created by God. But to become God's child, a person has to be born again *(John 1:12)*.
- God took His dear and beloved Son and allowed Him to be crucified so we would not perish in Hell. He did it so we would become His legitimate children.
- As an earthly father, everything beneficial that I do for my children is filtered through love, even if it causes me to make great sacrifices.
- It is the Father's nature to watch over us, correct us and steer us into safety *(Proverbs 3:11–12)*.
- Our Father God loves us with an everlasting love, and draws us close with loving kindness.
- Discipline, in God's view, is not to destroy but correct and redirect.
- Father God does not want us to live in anxiety but in rest and confidence in His ability to meet our needs. In Psalm 3, David says that he enjoys peaceful sleep, knowing that when he wakes, God is there to meet his needs.
- Fathers ought to speak blessings over their children and affirm them.

==

"God's blessings go beyond anything we could ever dream."

Quotes.com

==

Chapter 4: Love Covenant — God of Blessing

God's love is very strong and contagious. God is very generous with His gifts. He is a God of blessing. He loves to *fully satisfy*. Has God ever done something for you that you least expected? It took you by surprise and left you elated. I remember a friend and work colleague handing me a set of car keys and telling me her seven-seater car was now mine. Talk about surprise! I was not expecting this huge gift. I had been trying to save up money at the time to purchase a car of my own. God knew I needed it, and so touched her heart and she released the car to me. There is purpose attached to God's blessings.

God blesses to bring us joy. For example, Hanna was barren and suffered ridicule from her husband's second wife, Peninnah. But God healed her womb and she received her miracle baby Samuel, who became a great prophet *(1 Samuel 1:20)*. After Samuel, she had five more children.

God blesses to show forth His power and glory. For example, God parted the Red Sea so that His people (the Israelites) could escape from Pharaoh and his army *(Exodus 14:21–22)*.

God blesses to get our attention. For example, consider Moses and the burning bush. Moses was amazed that a bush was on fire, yet it was not consumed or burnt up by the fire. While he drew closer out of curiosity, God spoke to him from out of the burning bush *(Exodus 3:1–4)*.

God blesses to change our direction in life. For example, think of Paul's Damascus Road experience. Paul was a Hebrew scholar who went around dragging believers to prison. At other times he stood as witness in support of the stoning to death of believers. One day, on his way to Damascus, which is the present-day capital city of Syria, Paul, then called Saul, had a tangible and life-changing encounter with Jesus. He went from persecuting believers to preaching the very same Gospel they preached *(Acts 9:1–6)*.

One of the first things God did after creating Adam and Eve was bless them. In this blessing, He said, *"Be fruitful and multiply; fill the earth, and subdue it; have dominion over the fish of the sea, over the birds of the air, and over every living thing that moves on the earth" (Genesis 1:27–28 NKJV)*. God gave Adam and Eve the power to rule, to command, to manage and to facilitate growth and increase. This happens to us in every area of life, whether it is having children, cultivating crops, developing technology or in the field of art and creativity. God's agenda for every person is to see them thrive, not just survive.

Back in Biblical history, God set out to meet a man who did not even know Him, nor cared to seek or worship Him. Yet God took interest in this man to begin a relationship, a love walk, a covenant. God had a plan to bless all nations of the earth through this one man. So God spoke to Abraham, who had never heard the Father's voice before.

God is not hiding from us. He wants to reveal more of Himself to us, just like He did to the patriarchs of old *(1 Corinthians 2:10)*. God revealed Himself to the prophets *(Amos 3:7)*.

God divinely interrupted Abraham's life and presented to him what we have come to understand as a *covenant*. It is called the Abrahamic covenant, initiated by God. *Genesis 12* opens up with a title: *God Calls Abraham.* The first thing God says to Abraham is, *"Leave where you are and journey to where I show you to go."* This required a certain level of faith. Abraham was being asked to put his belief and trust in a God he had just met. It was Abraham's first encounter, but certainly not God's, for He knew exactly who Abraham was. The Bible says God is the One who knit us together while we were in the womb *(Jeremiah 1:5)*. God told Jeremiah that He had a purpose for his life even before he was born. God had a purpose for all our lives even before we set foot on the planet *(Ephesians 1:4–5)*.

After initiating conversation with Abraham, God immediately promised to bless him and establish him in greatness. *"I will make you a great nation; I will bless you and make you great; And you shall be a blessing. I will bless those who bless you, And I will curse him who curses you; And in you all the families of the earth shall be blessed" (Genesis 12:2–3 NKJV).*

It is amazing that God showed up and promised to bless Abraham in such a powerful way even though Abraham was clueless as to who this God really was. Abraham grew up in the land of Ur of the Chaldees where idol-worship was the norm. When it comes to idols and false gods, their worshippers are the ones doing everything for them. These idols are lifeless, made with human hands. But our true and living God does more for us than we could ever hope to do for Him. Our God is the only God who died for us and rose again to give us eternal life. Our God is the only God who promised us new glorified bodies that will never die or be sick.

Our God is the only God who promised us true peace and joy, and He promised us mansions and streets of gold in Heaven.

Abraham obeyed and departed as God had asked him to. When we step in God's direction we open ourselves up to His storehouse of blessing. God never approaches us empty-handed. When He approached Abraham, He came with a covenant that was loaded with blessing. In *Genesis 13*, when Abraham had moved to Hebron, God spoke to him and told him He would give him land and also multiply his offspring. They would be so many, it would be hard to count them *(Genesis 13:15–16)*. This promise of blessing of children was communicated to Abraham before he had his son Isaac.

Abraham was old and Sarah was barren. That barren condition did not bother God. He still promised them a son, because He has the power to bring His promises to pass. When the time was right, He turned that barrenness into fertility. When the angel Gabriel appeared to Zechariah, he announced that a son would be born to him and his wife Elizabeth, and that the child's name would be called John. Even though Zechariah doubted this promise as he and Elizabeth were old, the angel Gabriel assured Zechariah that the promise would be fulfilled at the appointed time. Elizabeth fell pregnant and gave birth to John the Baptist who was Jesus' forerunner. God calls those things that are not as though they were *(Romans 4:17)*.

In *Genesis 15,* Abraham was concerned that he had no heir. He even suggested to God that his steward Eliezer would end up inheriting his blessing and heritage. God reiterated the promise of a son to Abraham. I believe God was reassuring him and stamping out doubt. The Bible says God brought Abraham out of his tent and told him his offspring would be more than the stars in the sky. God was not going to change His mind.

Even after Sarah gave her maidservant Hagar to Abraham to have a child on their behalf, God still kept His word and gave them their own son Isaac who would be their heir. The angel of the Lord said to Sarah, *"Is anything too hard for the LORD? At the time appointed I will return unto you, according to the time of life, and Sarah shall have a son" (Genesis 18:14 NKJV).*

The covenant that God made with Abraham was not limited to his lifetime. God had already spoken to Abraham about blessing his seed, and consequently, all the nations of the earth. No one can exhaust God's blessings. So, when we ask, we should ask big. Physically and spiritually, God has unsearchable riches *(Ephesians 3:8)*. God's resources cannot be depleted. God will always have more than we need.

There came a time in Abraham and Sarah's life when God changed their names. These signified that God was bringing a shift in their lives. They were about to transition from barrenness to fruitfulness, from less to plenty, from obscurity to prominence. God was conditioning their thinking. He was lifting their expectation even in their season of waiting. Abraham was originally Abram before God changed his name to Abraham in accordance with all He had promised to do in his life. Abraham means *father of a multitude,* or *exalted father.* He changed Sarah's name from Sarai to Sarah, which means *princess.* This is quite amazing. God, being King, calls her princess. God initiated them into His royal family. Consequently, the Bible calls us kings and priests *(Revelation 1:6)*.

In *Genesis 13:2*, the Bible says that Abraham was very rich. God was the one responsible for the wealth increase in his life. That is the power of covenanting with God. We get what He has. We get His goodness. We get His power and anointing. We get His love and protection. We get His glorious riches — after all, we are the King's kids.

Why does God love to bless? Why is God so generous? I believe He does it for three reasons: one, He has the ability to bless; two, it is in His nature; and three, He gets great joy out of blessing humanity. Paul, the apostle puts us in remembrance of the powerful words of Jesus when He says, *"It is more blessed to give than to receive" (Acts 20:35 NKJV)*. Personally, I am not so troubled by my problems because I am way too busy counting my blessings. God is the One I thank because His signature is all over my blessings. Too many people are looking at what the enemy is doing. They are overly concerned with their troubles. It is high time we looked at God. We ought to expect great things from Him. We ought to change our focus from the problems to the problem-solver. Problems have an expiration date, but blessings are everlasting. God is so good that in His presence troubles turn to solutions and curses are negated by His blessings.

When we are in trouble, one word from God can swing it all around for our good. Esther, an orphaned Jewish girl who ended being chosen by the Persian King Ahasuerus as bride, risked her life going before the king when it was not the appropriate time to, but the king showed her favour. *"the king held out to Esther the golden scepter that was in his hand" (Esther 5:2 NKJV)*. Normally, if someone went before the King without being summoned, they could be executed or pardoned. Queen Esther went before King Ahasuerus to plead the case of her people, the Israelites, who were in danger of extermination by evil Haman. Haman was a vizier in the Persian Empire under King Ahasuerus. He hated and opposed the Israelites and wanted them annihilated. In the end, the Israelites were saved, and Haman and his ten sons were executed. His own evil plot cost him and his family their lives *(Esther 7)*. God knows how to deal with our enemies. He fights on our behalf and lets us enjoy the victory *(1 Samuel 17:47)*. Children of the covenant are automatically children of blessing. There are many things in my household that my children get to enjoy just by virtue of being my children. We are of the household of God, so start to expect and enjoy the Father's blessings.

Perhaps you are facing something difficult or life-threatening. Stay in faith and believe God. He has a *turn-around* for you that will dissolve that issue. God knows how to bring you through. *"When you pass through the waters, I will be with you; And through the rivers, they shall not overflow you. When you walk through the fire, you shall not be burned, Nor shall the flame scorch you, For I am the Lord your God, The Holy One your God"* (Isaiah 43:2–3 NKJV).

Despite the intensity of the trial, we must count our blessings and keep our focus on God, for only then will we see the greatness of God in every situation and His ability to rescue us from all snares and traps. On the other hand, let our struggles solidify our faith in our unchanging God. He did not give us life and energy to waste it on worry. Rather, we ought to use our strength to praise God and do His great work. Heaven is backing us. Greater is Jesus who is in us than Satan in the world *(1 John 4:4)*.

God does not wait for us to be perfect or super-spiritual in order to bless us. All God needs is half a chance to bless us. God has been working on our behalf long before we became aware. He is willing to make a way for us out of the mess, even if we have caused that mess. In view of this, let us work with Him, not against Him. Let us get our stubborn wills out of the way and surrender to God's divine and loving care. God is able to take better care of us than we can of ourselves.

God is so good, that when He blesses us, He removes sorrow from the equation so we can fully enjoy the blessing. *"The blessing of the LORD makes one rich, And adds no sorrow with it" (Proverbs 10:22 NKJV).* God is not in the business of sorrow, but pleasure and delight. He let Jesus take all our sin, sorrow and punishment on the cross. When we experience sorrow, just remember, weeping may endure for the night but joy comes in the morning time *(Psalm 30:5).* God has a bright and glorious morning for us that will make the sorrow-filled night insignificant.

We cannot enjoy the benefits of God's covenant if we do not accept it. God's covenant is one of peace, not strife and pain *(Numbers 25:12).* God deals in everlasting terms because He is eternal. He is from everlasting to everlasting *(Psalm 90:2).* He will not break His covenant. He remains forever mindful of it *(Psalm 111:5).* God's covenant of love, peace and blessing is a gift to us. However, gifts have to be received and used, or else we can never truly benefit from them.

God is the God of abundance. He did not just supply Abraham and Sarah's needs, but gave them more than they needed. God does not bless according to our riches, but according to His. He desired to perpetuate His glorious blessings from generation to generation through Abraham and Sarah. God is wealthy beyond measure. Some people believe that it is not right for believers to be wealthy. They think that poverty is a sign of godliness or holiness. That is absurd. The Bible itself is full of verses that show that God wants us to be blessed. God placed gold and other minerals in the earth for our use*(Genesis 2:11–12).* He made Abraham very rich *(Genesis 13:2).* He gave Solomon great wealth, saying, *"I will give you riches and wealth and honour, such as none of the kings have had who were before you, nor shall any after you have the like" (1 Chronicles 1:12 NKJV).* Solomon was the richest man who ever lived. The Devil did not make him rich; it was God. Poverty is one of the most ungodly things on the planet. God blesses people with great wealth so they can use it and also help others less fortunate with it. God has no issue with our having riches so long as wealth does not possess or control us and distance us from Him.

God does not take away His blessings and gifts from us. People work themselves out of blessing by what they choose to do. For example, when God blesses someone with a beautiful car or job, and they crash that car or lose that job because of drunkenness or unreliability, they have themselves to blame. Receiving the blessings is one thing; being responsible with them is quite another. We have to adhere to some disciplines and safeguards regarding our lives and gifts in order to maintain and maximise who we are.

The gifts God gives are permanent in our lives *(Romans 11:29)*. Some people bury their gifts and remain unfruitful. It is like being a gifted singer or teacher, but not putting that gift to use. God's gifts in our lives are not for dormancy but are for activity. A farmer may be blessed with much land, but if he does nothing with it, the only harvest he will get is weeds. The apostle Paul encourages us to stir up the gifts that are in us *(2 Timothy 1:6)*. Gifts have a purpose — and burial is not a justifiable option. Reading the Parable of the Talents in the twenty-fifth chapter of the Gospel of Matthew, we quickly realize that God loves us to be efficient, fruitful and profitable with whatever abilities He entrusted us with. No one can benefit from a buried gift. God gave us gifts out of the goodness of His heart. The outworking and full benefit of those gifts happen when we exercise those gifts.

God promised to give us the power to get wealth. *Deuteronomy 8:18 says, "And you shall remember the LORD your God, for it is He who gives you power to get wealth, that He may establish His covenant which He swore to your fathers" (NKJV)*. The Bible says that the blessing of Abraham comes on the Gentiles *(Galatians 3:14)*. God did not restrict His power and blessing to the Jews only. He grafted us into it.

God wants us to get the best out of life. We are encouraged to pursue with passion the best things in life. However, in our pursuit of greatness, let us remain humble, and remember to spread love, peace and joy. Love builds, love unites, love forgives, love supports, love endures, and love is selfless *(1 Corinthians 13:4–13)*.

Jesus is our mediator of a better covenant that He purchased for us with His precious blood *(Hebrews 8:6; 12:24)*. We enter in or become partakers of this covenant when we accept Him as Lord and Saviour. In accepting this covenant, God becomes ours and we become His. In this covenant we have access to God's healing, deliverance, wealth, protection, peace, love, comfort, eternal life and so much more. I can confidently say that because of this covenant we have mansions prepared for us in Heaven. I can further say that because of this amazing covenant we are co-heirs with Christ. What a great inheritance! We are locked into this wonderful covenant of blessing, and Satan is locked out.

Once, we were strangers, like Abraham, until God reached out to us and brought us into His glorious covenant. As Paul wrote to the church in Ephesus, *"At that time you were without Christ, being aliens from the commonwealth of Israel and strangers from the covenant of promise, having no hope and without God in this world. But now in Christ Jesus you who once were far off have been brought near by the blood of Christ"* (Ephesians 2:12–13 *NKJV*). God's goodness has made all this possible for us!

God's covenant with us is not just a love covenant, but a blood covenant too. We must constantly value this covenant because it was established through the precious blood of Jesus Christ. It was not a cheap covenant. Jesus suffered terribly so we could enjoy the many spiritual and physical benefits of this sacred covenant. This really shows the goodness of God towards us.

King David, blessed and powered by God, wanted to do something good for those of the house of Saul. He sought out Jonathan's son, Mephibosheth. He did it because of the covenant between himself and Jonathan, even though Jonathan was dead *(1 Samuel 20:42)*. The covenant lives beyond the grave. At that time, Mephibosheth was in a place called Lo-debar. It was a place without pasture. It was barren and limited, which was symbolic of Mephibosheth's physical state. He was crippled in both feet. He was limited and almost forgotten. Have you ever felt that way, where nothing seemed great in your life and you felt limited in many ways? God has a plan to break you out of those limitations.

King David found Mephibosheth and invited him to stay in his palace where he enjoyed food and safety at the king's table. Everyone related to him came under this great blessing. Mephibosheth was not even born when his father Jonathan and David cut covenant, but here he was benefiting greatly from that covenant. He went from the *gutter-most* to *uppermost* because of the covenant. The covenant Jesus made with the Father on our behalf took us out of the darkness and muck and seated us in Heavenly places *(Ephesians 2:6)*. We are children of covenant, which entitles us to God's great blessings.

RECAP

- God loves to *fully satisfy*. God is skilled in the art of blessing. There is purpose attached to His blessings.
- God blesses us to bring us joy and to show forth His power and glory. He blesses us to get our attention and to change our direction in life.
- God divinely interrupted Abraham's life and presented him with a *covenant*. It is called the Abrahamic covenant.
- We are children of the new covenant that Jesus attained for us with His precious blood.
- Children of the covenant are automatically children of blessing.
- God knows how to deal with our enemies. He fights on our behalf and lets us enjoy the victory *(1 Samuel 17:47)*.
- God's blessings cannot be exhausted, so ask for big things. God has unsearchable riches *(Ephesians 3:8)*.
- Once, we were strangers, like Abraham, until God reached out to us and brought us into His glorious covenant.
- In this covenant we have access to God's healing, deliverance, wealth, protection, peace, love, comfort, everlasting life and so much more.
- The covenant Jesus made with the Father on our behalf took us out of the darkness and muck and seated us in Heavenly places *(Ephesians 2:6)*.

==

"God is a God of restoration. When we place the broken pieces of our lives in His hands, He restores them to a beauty that far outshines the former."

Pinterest.com

==

Chapter 5: The Robe, the Ring, the Shoes

Standing at the altar of the beautiful Durban Christian Centre Chapel in Durban, South Africa, I waited with constrained excitement. Anytime soon my bride-to-be would come walking down the aisle with her father in arm. That moment arrived. Everyone stood, taking in the view, as my beautiful bride walked gracefully down the aisle to the cue of a love ballad.

We all stood in awe. My heart swelled with love, joy and wonder! She looked so beautiful in her specially designed wedding dress and veil along with pearl earrings, a gold watch and gold wedding shoes. My *Cinderella* had arrived. I was enchanted. Everything about her was perfect. She was dressed so rightly for this occasion, and looked gorgeous. Our skilled photographer managed to capture all of that beauty.

Seventeen years later, I still have moments where I stare at a framed photo of her in our living room. She still has the dress in her closet. One day I asked her if she would slip back into it and marry me again when we reach our twentieth year. She laughed and said, *"I doubt I would fit into it."*

There is something wonderful about being properly and gorgeously attired for whatever occasion we attend. It signifies that we have understood the nature of the event. We have thought about the best outfit for it. We are interested in looking our best at the event. We do not want to be an embarrassment at the event.

I took my wife to watch the latest version of *Beauty and the Beast* at our local cinema. Belle (Emma Watson), a beautiful and independent young lady, is taken prisoner by Dan Stevens' portrayal of the Beast in his ice-frozen and deserted castle. Her ability to look beyond the beast's hideous exterior and see his kind heart breaks the spell that has bound the otherwise handsome prince in this hideous form and brings warmth and life back to the palace. My wife and I found ourselves truly enthralled by this 2017 American romantic musical with its dazzling scenes. I particularly admired Belle's beautiful, yellow-silk ball gown and dazzling jewels. Even more so was her wedding attire towards the end of the musical. She looked stunning and well suited for the occasion in her royal celebration gown. She was dressed just right for this occasion. This goes beyond just necessity to include beauty, style and taste. We call it fashion and beauty. People want to look amazing for the occasions they attend.

Have you ever turned up at an event in the totally wrong clothing? It is quite embarrassing. You feel out of place. No one in their right mind intentionally shows up at a wedding dressed in a tracksuit or shorts and T-shirt (with the exception of beach weddings in swelteringly hot countries). Rather, ladies turn up in beautiful dresses and men in sharp suits or tuxedos to fit the occasion, and they enjoy the occasion.

God created Adam and placed him in Eden. He then created Eve in Eden. God dressed them in righteousness, making them rulers and dominators. We can only imagine how beautiful and perfect they were. They were covered in glory and royalty, since God is royalty and is King. Through relationship and the gift of righteousness they had access to His power and presence. They were dressed right to have daily encounters with their Heavenly Father. But this all changed when they lost their righteous garments or covering. What went wrong?

Initially, they had an invitation, so to speak, from God the King, and the correct dress to the occasion of everlasting life, blessing, peace, joy and fellowship was righteousness. However, an enemy came into the Garden of Eden and invited them to a different occasion. He fooled them into thinking it would be bright and glorious, but it was dark and cursed. They exchanged their righteous garments for Satan's sinful and wretched attire through their act of disobedience. Now they were dressed right for sin, but unsuited for innocence and perfection.

Thus, the Fall of Man began. Adam and Eve were now dressed for what they really did not want: *sickness, death, strife, toil and spiritual death.* They were deceived, and went from a celebration event with God to the tormenting clutches of Satan, the fallen prince (ruler) of this world *(John 16:11).* Mankind now bears the image of fallen Adam and Eve. But God sent the second Adam (Jesus) to redeem us so we could now have the image of the Heavenly prince, King and Saviour. *1 Corinthians 15:47–49 says, "The first man [Adam] was of the earth, made of dust; the second Man [Jesus] is the Lord from Heaven. As was the man of dust, so also are those who are made of dust; and as is the Heavenly Man, so also are those who are Heavenly [regenerated in spirit]. And as we have borne the image of the man of dust, we shall also bear the image of the Heavenly Man" (NKJV).* All that is corrupt will be replaced by incorruptibility, according to *1 Corinthians 15:53*.

Adam and Eve ran off and hid when God showed up in the Garden. They felt naked and ashamed. If I dropped you in the middle of a wedding celebration in your PJs, or completely naked for that matter, you would run for the nearest exit, completely embarrassed. But if I dropped you in that celebratory event in a suitable and attractive outfit, you would not be embarrassed. You would be more inclined to stay and enjoy the event.

While I may seem to be just caught up with attire, I can assure you I know that people are far more important than what they wear. Even though Adam and Eve lost their righteousness, and plunged the rest of humanity into this same pitiful state of unrighteous dress, God had a plan to re-dress us, because we are more important than what we lost.

Adam and Eve collected a bunch of fig leaves and sewed garments for themselves. They were attempting to re-dress so they would be suitable for their encounter with God. Dress code is determined by the one who initiated the event, not the attendees. God rejected Adam and Eve's fig-leaf attire as it fell short of His standard. It did not match His righteous standard. Man's efforts to self-right hardly turn out successful. *Isaiah 64:6* says, *"We are all like an unclean thing, And all our righteousness are like filthy rags. We all fade as a leaf, And our iniquities, like the wind, have taken us away" (NKJV).* If their fig-leaf garments were suitable, they would not have hidden away from God. The righteousness that they lost could be restored only by God because it came from Him. The Lord is our righteousness *(Jeremiah 23:6).* The fig leaves they used to cover themselves would eventually turn brown and crumble because they had no life flowing through them. Just like Jesus touched and healed the man with the withered hand, only He can undo the withered things in our lives and bring wholeness.

Jesus came into the world as light to bring mankind out of darkness. Unfortunately, because people loved darkness and had become so comfortable with sin, they hid or rejected the light *(John 1:5, 11).* It is like refusing to see the doctor when you are very ill. God cannot help people who reject Him and His Word. While God wants to wash them and rid them of their stinking sinful garments, they rebel and prefer the sinful and soiled garments of this life. *"The wise men are ashamed, They are dismayed and taken. Behold, they have rejected the word of the LORD; So what wisdom do they have?" (Jeremiah 8:9 NKJV).*

God clothed Adam and Eve with skins. He was letting them know that the price of re-dressing them in righteousness would be His responsibility. This act of covering was the foreshadowing of what Jesus would come and do on the cross for mankind. *"For He (God) made Him (Jesus) who knew no sin to be sin for us, that we might become the righteousness of God in Him" (2 Corinthians 5:21 NKJV).*

Adam and Eve did not pay for their original righteous state. It came from God. That is why God gave it back to us as a gift *(Romans 5:17)*. Righteousness cannot be earned by human effort. The fig leaves that Adam and Eve wore were unable to clothe them with Godly righteousness and could not appease their sinful conscience. They still felt shame. They still felt naked and fearful.

Jesus told many parables that had a great practical and spiritual significance. In one such parable, found in *Luke 15:11–24*, which ultimately details the father's love, a wealthy father had two sons. The younger son demanded from his father his share of the inheritance that the father had for them. Not too long after acquiring his share of the wealth, he left for a faraway country. He pushed his family out of his life. There are many who just want what God can provide but make no room for Him in their lives until trouble comes knocking.

Lacking wisdom, this son soon found himself in want. He spent all his wealth on things that gave him temporal pleasure with no proper forecast for the future. The proper use of the knowledge, prudence and self-control God gives us will help prevent shipwreck of our lives. *Luke 15:13* says, *"the younger son gathered all together* [his wealth] *journeyed to a far country, and there wasted his possessions with prodigal* [wasteful] *living" (NKJV).* The pleasures of this world are only for a moment. This son did not invest his wealth or help the poor or start a business to perpetuate his wealth. Eve seemed caught up only in the moment, not thinking of the consequences when she ate the forbidden fruit *(Genesis 3)*. Similarly, the lost son seemed only interested in immediate gratification.

The lost son became destitute and ended up working for someone else. The nature of his job was to mind pigs in the field. For a Jewish son, pigs were viewed as unclean. He was so desperate for shelter, food and clothing that working with the pigs was the only option to stay alive *(Luke 15:14–16).*

A series of bad choices and lack of wisdom landed him where he least expected to be, just like the first son Adam landed up in sin and darkness, outside of Eden where he least expected to be.

At times, the lost son was so hungry, even the pigs' food seemed inviting. The Bible says that no one helped him. No one can help us out of sin, but God. The Bible says he came to his senses, saying, *"How many of my father's hired servants have bread enough and to spare, and I perish with hunger!" (Luke 15:17 NKJV).* As God's children, why should we stay lost and destitute outside His Kingdom, while His angels (servants) have plenty, and enjoy His blessings and presence and light? One first has to realize one's wretched state, and then seek a way out. Jesus said He is the way, the truth and the life *(John 14:6).* Through truth and love, Jesus (the Word) becomes a lamp unto our feet and a light unto our path.

God is waiting with open arms for us to return to Him. We all must return to God our Father for help. The lost son made the first wise decision. He went back home to his father. *"I will arise and go to my father, and I will say to him, Father, I have sinned against heaven, and before you" (Luke 15:18 NKJV).* This was a step in the right direction. We have to acknowledge our sinful state and ask God to forgive us and receive cleansing through the shed blood of Jesus.

The lost son made his way back home. While he was some distance away from his father's home, his father saw him afar off approaching and had compassion on him. God has great compassion for us. The father did not even wait for his lost son to reach home. He ran out to meet him, hugged him and kissed him *(Luke 15:20).* The lost son had not expected to be greeted with such love and compassion from his father. The first thing he said was, *"Father, I have sinned against heaven and in your sight, and am no longer worthy to be called your son" (Luke 15:21 NKJV).* We may have felt unworthy, but God has made us worthy by letting Jesus take our sin and punishment on the cross.

I love how the father responded. He did not even entertain the idea of turning his son into a slave. He received him back as a son. God did not redeem us to enslave us. He freed us to be His legitimate sons. The father said to his servant, *"Quick! Bring out the best robe and put it on him, and put a ring on his finger and sandals on his feet" (Luke 15:23, NIV).* I love that the father said, "Quick." When we repent, God does not wait, but immediately forgives and restores.

Allow me to unpack the significance of these three items of wear that the father bestowed on his son.

THE ROBE

I believe the lost son must have sold his nice sandals, garments and whatever jewellery he left with. Now he returns in a faded and old beggar-like robe (garment) and probably no shoes on his feet, all his fancy apparel gone. His condition spoke volumes. He was in dire need. The new robe he now received from his father is symbolic of the righteous covering we received at the point of our spiritual rebirth. The son could not afford this. He had to receive it as a gift from his father. We could not afford God's righteousness. He gave it to us as a gift. The lost son had to surrender his pitiful and corrupt ways and thinking in order to avail himself of the good gifts his father had for him. Gaining Christ is a win, not a loss. Losing our self-righteousness (filthy rags) for God's righteousness is a huge gain. Paul was ready to strip himself of all his previous religious piety. He said, *"I have suffered the loss of all things, and count them as rubbish, that I may gain Christ and be found in Him, not having my own righteousness, which is from the law, but that which is through faith in Christ, the righteousness which is from God by faith" (Philippians 3:8–9 NKJV).* God does not require us to work for righteousness, but to receive it freely as a gift.

The lost son's image was being transformed. Gone was the old tattered garment he arrived in. The lost son was being re-dressed to look like a son, not a slave or beggar. God does not want us clothed in sin, in poverty, in depression, in shame or brokenness. God clothes us with garments of salvation and covers us with robes of righteousness *(Isaiah 61:10).* No wonder He said He would give us a garment of praise in place of a spirit of heaviness *(Isaiah 61:3).* Powerful words in Isaiah 52:1–2 say, *"Awake, awake, Zion, clothe yourself with strength! Put on your garments of splendour, Jerusalem, the holy city … shake off your dust; rise up, sit enthroned, Jerusalem" (NIV).* It is time for families and nations to submit to God and be dressed in dignity and integrity. No family or nation can thrive as God intended if they remain in corruption and depravities of all kinds. While God accepts us as we are when we come to Him, He will not leave us as we are. He begins a work of transformation immediately, just like we see the lost son's father transforming him.

The lost son, who represents lost humanity and Israel, was redeemed without money *(Isaiah 52:3)*. It cost the father to redeem his lost son, just like it cost God our Father to redeem us. It was expensive — it cost God the precious blood of His Son Jesus. As I have pointed out before, the Bible says that we were not redeemed with corruptible things, but with the precious blood of Jesus that had no blemishes *(1 Peter 1:18–19)*.

God does not clothe us partially. He operates in full measures. Our redemption was a full package. Through His manifold wisdom, He weaves His goodness intricately in our lives *(Ephesians 3:10–12)*. Let us continue to put on the best God has to offer.

THE RING

A few years into our marriage, my wife and I pawned our wedding rings due to dire financial need. It was a sad moment, as these were very expensive rings that meant so much to us both. When our finances improved, I bought my wife another beautiful wedding ring. Sometime later she replaced mine with a beautiful one, too. Unfortunately, I lost it and could not find it. This happened twice. In the year 2017, I decided I was going to buy another one and make sure it did not get lost. You see, I always take off my ring whenever I wash dishes or bathe, or when I am doing some messy manual task. That is how I lost them.

In November of 2017, Paul Ewart, a friend of mine who owns a jewellery store, contacted me and offered me a free wedding ring. He said he felt God leading him to do this for me. I was thrilled! My wife and I drove up to his jewellery store in Armagh in Northern Ireland. Together we selected this attractive gold ring. The ring looked beautiful on my finger and felt right and complete. My friend Paul prayed together with us as we blessed the ring. God works in wonderful ways. My wife cautioned me really to take care of this ring and not lose it. Our rings are a special symbol of our union and commitment to each other.

After clothing his lost son with a new robe, the father had a ring placed on his finger. What was the significance behind this? When Joseph was put in a position of power by Pharaoh, we see Pharaoh placing a ring on his finger. *"So Pharaoh said to Joseph, 'I hereby put you in charge of the whole land of Egypt.' Then Pharaoh took his signet ring off his finger and put it on Joseph's finger"* *(Genesis 41:41–42, NIV)*. That ring symbolized power and authority. It spoke of the powerful position of prominence that Joseph was elevated to as ruler. Bear in mind that prior to this Joseph had been relegated to the position of a slave and prisoner.

When the lost son's father put a ring on his finger, he was giving him back his authority and position as a son and ruler in his household. Originally, before the Fall, Adam and Eve had this status. God had given them authority and rule over the earth *(Genesis 1:26–28)*. The signet ring set Joseph apart as ruler, just like the lost son's new ring set him apart from his previous self-induced enslaved life. God has given us power and authority over Satan and every demon and evil spirit. God has restored us as sons in His Kingdom. Jesus, who has all power and authority, has empowered us to rule and overcome and to carry out the purposes of God.

THE SHOES

My wife is a size three when it comes to shoes. She has small feet, and this is no exaggeration. The beautiful gold heels she wanted for the wedding could not be found in her size, so we asked a company to make a size three for her in that exact style. Most times she would shop in the children's department as some stores only catered for size four upwards when it came to adult sizes.

Shoes are important to us all, but, I think, especially to women. I have a friend, Desmond Paraboo, in South Africa who is the CEO of the Labora Shoe Factory his dad established in 1989. Most of the company's sales come from female shoes they manufacture. Ladies love shopping and shoes would be a priority.

My dad used to own a pair of Crocket and Jones shoes. Back then they were one of the most attractive and valued makes of shoes for men. They were expensive, too. I dreamed of owning a pair myself one day. To my surprise, in my final year of school, my dad bought me a pair of Crocket and Jones. I was "over the moon" with excitement. I wore them with such pride and confidence. But growing up in my pre-teen years, we could not afford more than one pair of shoes. All I had were my school shoes. This resulted in many foot injuries from running around and playing barefooted. I remember my older brother loaning me his pair of *Adidas* runners. I wore them to dress-up day at school with pride and joy. I enjoyed the compliments from my friends. I did not even want to take them off when I got home.

The lost son returned home without the beautiful and valued shoes he left with. He had probably sold them when he was in desperate need of food. His feet were dirty and probably bruised. His gracious father ordered new shoes for his feet after they were washed clean *(Luke 15:22)*. God has translated us into His Kingdom and given us a new walk. He has re-dressed our feet. Shoes symbolize protection, stability, movement and direction. God has clothed us for a new walk and new direction.

Previously, the son walked away from his father. He walked into trouble and depravity. There was a way that seemed right to him but it led to destruction. His foolishness led him astray *(Proverbs 12:15)*. God should not be blamed when we go astray. Applying God's wisdom leads us to a wholesome life. *"Let us walk in the light of the LORD" (Isaiah 2:5 NKJV)*. Eventually, the lost son made a decision to walk back to his father. That required humility and submission. Do not be afraid to walk back to God, for He is waiting with open arms.

The robe, the ring and the shoes were symbolic of restoration. The lost son was now cleansed, repositioned and empowered. He was accepted and restored as a son through the goodness of his father. Look what God our Heavenly Father has done for us. He is the lover of our souls. He has adopted us as sons. We are accepted in His beloved Kingdom *(Ephesians 1:6)*.

The lost son's father then declared a time of feasting and celebration in honour of his returned son. The lost son was now found, no longer lost in sin, greed and self. It was time to rejoice. We are told in Scripture that angels rejoice in Heaven every time someone accepts Jesus as Lord and Saviour. Heaven throws a party. One day we will all be there and there will be more partying. God loves a good time. There will be much reason to celebrate. God is happy about our redemption. We ought to enjoy it, too.

RECAP

- God created Adam and Eve and dressed them in righteousness and placed them in Eden, making them rulers and dominators.
- Through relationship and the gift of righteousness they had access to His power and presence. They were dressed right to have daily encounters with their Heavenly Father.
- They exchanged their righteous garments for Satan's sinful and wretched attire through their act of disobedience.
- The fig leaves that Adam and Eve wore were unable to clothe them with Godly righteousness and could not appease their sinful conscience.
- The lost son made his first wise decision: to go back home to his father. We all must return to God our Father for help. He is waiting with open arms for us to return to Him.
- The new robe the lost son received from his father symbolises the righteous covering we received upon our spiritual rebirth. We cannot afford God's righteousness — it is a gift.
- By putting a ring on his son's finger, the father was giving his son back his authority and position as heir and ruler. Adam had this status before the Fall.
- The father ordered new shoes for his son *(Luke 15:22)*. God has translated us into His Kingdom and given us a new walk. He has re-dressed our feet to walk in righteous paths.

===================================

"To trust God in the light is nothing, but to trust Him in the dark – **that is faith.** *"*

C.H. Spurgeon

===================================

Chapter 6: God in Your Dark Place

When my eldest son was three, he started feeling afraid of sleeping in the dark, so each night we had to leave the light on for him. Curious to know why, I asked the obvious question: *"Why are you afraid to sleep in the dark, son?"* He replied, *"The boogie man is going to get me."* For those who are not familiar with the term "boogie man," it is a made-up story of a monster that comes after naughty children at night. My next question to him was, *"Who told you that?"* He mentioned that his aunty had. Apparently, she would scare him with this story when he misbehaved, in order to make him listen.

I am quite sure she meant no harm, but he believed her, and fear was the result. As a good parent, I counteracted this by telling him the boogie man was not real. I also told his aunt to stop scaring him with that story. For three weeks he still wanted the light on. Each time I would repeat that the boogie man story was fiction.

After about four weeks of this, I tucked him in one night only for him to tell me that I could turn the light off. I was quite surprised. You can guess what my question was: *"Are you sure you want the light off?"* He replied, *"Yes, dad. I'm not afraid any more. The boogie man is not real."* I was thrilled! Finally, he believed my words as opposed to his aunt's. Fear was defeated. My son felt safe in the dark.

What are the things that scare us, whether we are alone or even in a crowd? Many people dread the night or some circumstance. Perhaps they are facing a devastating situation such as a terminal illness or divorce. Perhaps the enemy has been whispering words of calamity in their ear. God wants us to hear and believe His Word that brings hope and light. Jesus is called the light of the world. Satan has a report of fear and dread that he wants us to believe, but we must believe the good report of the Lord that brings peace and hope. *Proverbs 15:30* says that *"a good report makes the bones healthy" (NKJV)*. I love how the Expanded Bible expresses it: *"Good news makes you feel better."*

When we know God is with us, we ought to be trusting and hopeful even in dark situations. King David said, *"Though I walk through the valley of the shadow of death, I will fear no evil; For You are with me" (Psalm 23:4 NKJV)*. Darkness does not mean the absence of God.

In *Genesis 1*, when the earth was dark and formless, God the Holy Spirit was right there. Can we see God in the dark? Yes, we can, through the eyes of faith.

God commanded light to come and light swallowed up the dark. Nothing in our lives can stay dark when God gets involved. Our light burns brighter even though the world is getting darker with its many evils. God's goodness will not leave us in darkness. That is why Jesus came into the world: to be the light *(John 1:4–5)*.

God promised He would never leave nor forsake us *(Hebrews 13:5)*. That is a promise. The God of the mountain is also the God of the valley. In other words, God is not with us only when life is going very well and we have no darkening situations, but also when we face tragedies and tribulations. Njabulo Nxulu, a friend of mine, said, "I would rather go through my pain with God than without Him." After being shot and nearly paralysed, his recovery was a slow and difficult process. His faith in God and the help and love of his mother galvanized his resolve to make a full recovery. Never let tragedy beat you down to a point where you cannot even see God any more and rise to the top.

A helper brings comfort, strength, joy, sustenance and companionship. Right in the beginning God understood this and provided Adam with a wife, Eve. God called her a helpmate *(Genesis 2:20–22)*. A helper is a blessing. Adam could not fulfil all God destined for him without his helpmate. How sad for those who have no help or support when they fall. *"Woe to him who is alone when he falls, For he has no one to help him up"* *(Ecclesiastes 4:10 NKJV)*. Two are better than one. If one falls, the other will lift him or her. We are not alone. God has surrounded us with family and friends. He Himself is our help. God's goodness will not allow Him to let us lumber through life without help. *Hebrews 13: 6 says, "The LORD is my helper; I will not fear. What can man do to me?" (NKJV)*.

If something or someone is causing our destruction, then that thing or person is not our helper. That is a category Satan falls into. He deceived Adam and Eve into believing that he was there for their good. Instead, he was there to deceive them. We really do not need to be influenced by those who try to lead us down crooked paths. Spiritually blind people cannot lead us into spiritual life and awakenings. Of the blind leaders, Jesus said, *"Leave them; they are blind guides. If the blind lead the blind, both will fall into a pit" (Matthew 15:14)*. It

71

is best to be led by the Holy Spirit, for He knows all things and knows where to take us. God can make a way even in the dark because He is Light. He is a way-maker, a yoke-breaker and a burden-bearer. When God shows up, doors open. When God shows up, death backs off. When God shows up, demons tremble and flee. God is developing something beautiful for us, even when we cannot see it. It is like developing negatives in the dark to produce a beautiful picture seen in the light.

While Paul and Silas were praising God in prison, bound in chains, God broke in and freed them. God inhabits the praises of His people *(Psalm 22:3)*. When we are in trouble or in a dark situation, we ought to release praise unto God and watch Him work powerfully on our behalf. Darkness hides when God approaches. The Bible says that God lives in unapproachable light *(1 Timothy 6:16)*. This means that the light emanating from God is so bright that natural eyes cannot behold it. Devils stay far from it, for it *blinds* them silly.

When the disciples were heading over to the other side of the lake, a fierce storm suddenly arose. But Jesus got up and calmed that storm *(Mark 4:35–41)*. When God is in the boat, it will not sink; it will not go under. The Jesus in us cannot be sunk. He makes us buoyant. The apostle Paul said, *"We are hard-pressed on every side, yet not crushed; we are perplexed, but not in despair; persecuted, but not forsaken; struck down, but not destroyed" (2 Corinthians 4:8–9 NKJV)*.

Lazarus was dead for four days in a dark tomb. Jesus still called him out. He came out alive. All things are possible with God *(Matthew 19:26)*. Jesus Himself was locked up in a dark tomb, dead. But on the third day He came back to life by the power of the Holy Spirit. He is the resurrection and the life *(John 11:25)*. Jesus took the sting and victory out of death. We, at times, may feel like we are imprisoned. We may feel like a dream or relationship is dead, but God specializes in bringing dead things to life again. He is in the restoration and renewal business. God restores what has been depleted in our lives *(Joel 2:25)*. Even if it has been burned to the ground, He can raise it up from the ash heap.

Being a leper in Biblical times was quite a tragic situation for anyone with leprosy. There was no cure. The lepers felt like outcasts. They could not be with their family and friends. They were relegated to the outskirts of the city or town. They depended on those compassionate enough to throw scraps of food to them. They lived in the shadows and in pain, as their bodies deteriorated. No one wanted to be close to them for fear of catching the dreaded disease. In that state hope seemed like a fantasy. They were slowly and painfully dying, and they knew it — unless, by some miracle, healing came.

In *Matthew 8:1–3* we see a leper coming to Jesus because he wanted to be made whole again. He must have somehow heard about the Saviour and the healing miracles that were taking place. He was tired of living a painful and dejected life. Faith must have risen in his heart, or he would not have asked Jesus to make him clean. He did not have to wait to be healed and come into the light before he could believe. Right there in his dark situation he started to have hope. We must not let dark situations diminish our hope. We must trust that things will turn out for our good. It does not matter how bad we think the situation is. We serve a God who turns messes into messages, miseries into ministries and tests into testimonies.

Jesus reached out and touched the leper and willingly healed him. Just one touch can mean so much. When my father died, I remember how my deputy principal, André Botha, came over to the house, and all he did was hug me for quite a while. I am not ashamed to say I wept like a baby. I needed someone to tell me it was going to be all right. These kinds of sorrows are not without hope. One day I will see my father alive and well in Heaven.

God is omniscient and omnipresent. Just because we may be in a dark place does not mean God is unaware of where we are and what we need. God knows where to find us. Joseph was in a pit, but God did not leave him. Daniel was in a lion's den, but God shut the mouths of the lions. The apostle John was banished to the island of Patmos, but God was with him. He did not perish. Right there on the Island of Patmos God gave him the book of Revelation. God knows how to communicate good to us while frustrating the wicked plans of the enemy.

In *Numbers 17:7–10*, God commanded all the priests to lay their rods in a pile in the temple. Aaron's dry rod budded and blossomed and produced almonds in the dark. This was an overnight miracle performed by God to prove Aaron as the chosen leader of the priesthood. God was able to bring life and sustenance to a dead rod; how much more to the dead things in your life?

If Aaron's rod could speak, it would tell of how hopeful it had been growing up as a young tree, waiting for the day it could produce fruit. That was its primary purpose as an almond tree. However, before it had a chance to produce it was cut down by its master and left to dry out in the sun. How devastating, especially since its master did not give an explanation for this sudden change. Then its master shaved it, removing all outer bark. Now stripped and reduced to a bare rod, this almond tree must have thought its purpose was over. Have you ever been in a place or condition that seemed to sap your strength and purpose in life?

Something then happened that gave the almond rod a flicker of hope. Its master began using it as a staff. The almond rod stayed strong for this new purpose and felt grateful to be used by its master. However, after some time, its master threw it on the ground behind a thick curtain along with a pile of other rods. That feeling of hopelessness and devastation returned. Surely this was its end. Was it going to be set on fire and reduced to ashes by its master along with all the other rods? Was this the end? When we think we have reached our end, God shows up with a miracle. In the dark behind that thick curtain God did a quick and miraculous work on the almond rod. The power of God flowed through it and it blossomed and developed ripe almonds all in one night *(Numbers 17:8)*. After losing its first and second purpose, it gained a third but even higher purpose. It would remain as a testimony in God's presence *(Numbers 17:10)*. God is not done with us yet. He has higher and greater things in store. God does wonders even in the dark *(Psalm 88:12)*. We must still remain hopeful even in despairing circumstances.

Samson was a child dedicated to God from birth. God had blessed him with special power and supernatural strength to overthrow the enemies of Israel. There were conditions that God put in place. Samson was never to have his hair cut. Secondly, he was never to drink alcohol, and thirdly, he was never to touch dead bodies. Through rebellion and carelessness, Samson broke these conditions, and thereby lost his power. He ended up with his eyes plucked out by his enemies, and he found himself grinding corn in a dark prison, mocked by the Philistines *(Judges 16:21)*. The warrior with supernatural strength from God was now in a dark, pitiful state. It is quite interesting to note that Samson's name means "like the sun". But here he was groping blindly in the dark. The sun seemed snuffed out in his life. This was a major setback. Nevertheless, in prison, his hair began to grow back and he called out to God for help *(Judges 16:22, 28)*. God gave him a comeback. We serve a merciful God who hears our cry. A new day dawned in Samson's life. He ended up killing more of his enemies in one instant than throughout his life.

When we find ourselves in dark places with no way out, we must call upon the Lord who is a very present help in times of need. God knows how to get us out of dark places. After all, He is light. *"God is light and in Him is no darkness at all" (1 John 1:5 NKJV)*. God sent the apostle Paul to preach the Gospel primarily to the Gentiles. The purpose for this was to open their eyes, in order to turn them from darkness to light, and from the power of Satan to God *(Acts 26:17–18)*. Satan loves to keep people in fear, doubt, sickness and evils of all kinds. God is constantly leading them out of such dark things into His glorious light. He is such a good God.

Many people look bright and alive, but their hearts are darkened with foolish ideas and philosophies and ways that violate God's laws *(Romans 1:21–22)*. They have no illumination until they abandon their dark understanding for the light the Word of God brings. *"For You are my lamp, O LORD; the LORD shall enlighten my darkness" (2 Samuel 22:29 NKJV)*.

God has called us to walk by faith, not by sight. This means that we must not be affected by what we see, but believe what God says or shows us. We can still walk by faith in the dark. Our faith in the Word of God lights the way for us, giving the light of His glory even in the darkest situation.

RECAP

- God wants us to hear and believe His Word, for it brings hope and light. Jesus is called the light of the world.
- Darkness does not mean the absence of God. In *Genesis 1*, when the earth was dark and formless, God the Holy Spirit was right there.
- God is working on our behalf even in the dark. He is a way-maker, a yoke-breaker and a burden-bearer.
- We must not let dark situations diminish our hope. We must trust that things will turn out for our good. It does not matter how bad we think the situation is.
- We may feel like a dream or relationship is dead, but God specializes in bringing dead things to life again. He is in the business of restoration and renewal. God restores what has been depleted in our lives *(Joel 2:25)*.
- It does not matter how bad we think the situation is. We serve a God who turns messes into messages, miseries into ministries and tests into testimonies.
- When we find ourselves in dark places with seemingly no way out, we must call upon the Lord who is a very present help in times of need.
- In the dark behind that thick curtain, God did a quick and miraculous work on the almond rod. It budded, blossomed and produced ripe almonds in one night. God is able to do sudden miracles in our lives even in the dark times.

=====================================

"I cannot do without God, my greatest comfort where no human can reach."

Dr. Peter Tsou

=====================================

Chapter 7: Comforter

Comfort is something we all love. No one really likes to be made uncomfortable or to be in awkward situations. Certain comforts are good for the soul. God understands comfort and our need for it more than we realize. The Bible calls Him the God of all comfort *(2 Corinthians 1:3)*. In fact, Jesus said, *"I will not leave you orphans; I will come to you" (John 14:18 NKJV)*.

God's comfort is like placing your head on a soft, warm pillow at night and falling into a peaceful sleep with no anxiety threatening your sanity. There is security and tranquillity in the comfort God provides. A baby finds comfort, love and protection in its mother or father's arms. God wants us to experience His comfort in His loving arms. God said to His children, the Israelites, *"As one whom his mother comforts, so I will comfort you; And you shall be comforted in Jerusalem" (Isaiah 66:13 NKJV)*. God had assigned Himself to fight for them, protect them and provide for them. He is doing the same for us.

Before Jesus left earth, He promised that He would send the Holy Spirit, whom He called the Comforter. "Comforter" conveys the meaning that He cares and understands, that He is ready to help, that He heals psychological and emotional wounds, and that He gives mental stability. He is powerful, yet gentle. He regulates His power with love. From time to time we do face harsh realities or go through trials and tribulations, so we need someone who can identify with us and undergird us when we have been weakened and frazzled by adversity.

Most believers recognise the power and anointing of the Holy Spirit, and this is good; however, I believe Jesus wanted us to also recognise the Spirit's gentle, caring and loving personality. The Holy Spirit can be soft and comforting to us, yet He is very strong. At the moment of our spiritual rebirth, He connects our spirit with God the Father, allowing us to experience intimacy with Him. He gives us a sense of belonging, letting us know that we are children of God: *you received the Spirit of adoption by whom we cry out, 'Abba, Father.' The Spirit Himself bears witness with our spirit that we are children of God" (Romans 8:15–16 NKJV)*. We become God's children through spiritual regeneration.

The Holy Spirit is God's promise, given as a gift to us. Our Comforter is the result of God's goodness. Having the Holy Spirit is

God's way of saying to us, *"I will never leave you, nor forsake you"* *(Hebrews 13:5 NKJV)*. Knowing that God is always with us is very comforting, especially when we face troubling situations or tragedies.

God works everything in our lives together for our good *(Romans 8:28)*. God wants us to be in harmony with Him. As I have mentioned in the introduction, God calls things good when they please Him and are one with or in unity with His character. God called creation good, because it was in harmony or pleasing to Him. God created mankind and called us a good creation. If something is not in harmony with God, He does not see it as good and it will never get His endorsement. The disharmony it causes or lack of self-reflection it offers are two of the reasons why God will one day rid sin from the world completely. In fact, God is going to create a brand new earth *(Revelation 21:10)*. True comfort is born out of relationship and trust in God. There is comfort for the soul that loves the presence of God. Many good things happen in God's presence: for example, we are nourished and replenished in God's presence; we are accepted in His presence; and we are filled with His peace and joy. We love to be around people who make us feel loved, peaceful and accepted. We feel relaxed and at ease around them. We enjoy their company. Children feel safe and loved in the presence of their parents where, ideally, love, joy and protection are constantly communicated to them. Jesus was limited in His human body. He could not be in every place at the same time. He was contained. But the Holy Spirit can be everywhere at the same time and can offer comfort, power and encouragement to all at the same time. Being in harmony with God will produce comfort and joy. Our lives are like puzzles. God knows each piece of the puzzle and how they all fit, even when we do not know. It is truly comforting to know that God has not left us to figure it all out on our own. Our Comforter guides us and leads us into all truth. He shows us what is right and beneficial. He nudges us in the right path.

Someone who is a paramedic has the primary role of coming to the aid of the injured. We see it especially when there has been an accident. Paramedics are the first responders to treat and stabilize and provide comfort for the person or people in need. The prefix *para* (borrowed from Greek) means to *"come alongside, to be near or be beside"*. Without paramedics many people would not make it to hospital alive.

The Holy Spirit acts in a similar way when we need help. He remains with us to help. His other name is Helper. Since the Holy Spirit is God, it is appropriate to say that God is our Helper. The Geek word is *paraklétos*. It means *counsellor, helper, comforter and assistant*. *Klétos* means *called or divinely appointed*. When we combine *para* and *klétos* we see that the Holy Spirit was divinely appointed or called to be beside us. He is also within us.

No one wants to experience tragedy, but when it does happen, we have God on our side. Help is closer than we can imagine — God the Holy Spirit, our greatest paramedic, is ever present. Tebita Ambulance Service in Ethiopia was started by Kibrel Adebe, triggered by a tragic accident he witnessed that involved a twelve-year-old girl. It affected him to such a degree that he was moved to offer this paramedic service. Even out of tragedy comes good. After acquiring his licence, Kibrel sold his own house to purchase the first three of his fifteen ambulances. With a substantial staff, they provide services to people with medical conditions or injuries due to various causes. When we help others, we are partnering with God in bringing comfort to them.

Some comforts are bad for us. It may sound like a paradox, but it is not. There are comforts we gravitate towards that are hindrances to us. Some gravitate towards excessive food consumption, junk food or excessive alcohol, or other negative addictions. Some comforts are not sin but can become obstacles if they slow or hinder our growth. They may be familiarities or habits we circle around.

Peter left the comfort place of the boat to walk on water. The boat was a safe place of comfort for the disciples, which was not a bad thing. However, Peter got to experience what the rest did not because he was willing to leave that comfort zone.

When a comfort zone stunts further growth or expansion, it needs to be discarded. An eagle upsets the nest and throws out her young in an effort to cause them to fly and mature. They may think she is cruel, but she is helping them realize their inner potential. They were designed to fly, to soar. Later, what seemed like discomfort will become comfort on a new level. We often look back with gratitude towards the people who challenged us or forced us out of our comfort zones where potential was being stifled.

God is a good parent. He will not allow our comforts to stifle our progress. We have to make the uncomfortable sacrifices that lead to greater levels of progress. Feeling challenged and stretched is good. A bow is meant to be stretched far back for the arrow to hit its intended target effectively with necessary force. Muscles do not develop without exercise. God will use various things to push us out of our comfort zones so we can grow. The best way we can grow is to step out of our comfort zones. We are not prone to welcome the unfamiliar, but as children of God we can push ourselves beyond new challenges and step into a whole new world of opportunities. It may be the new area you moved into that opens up new opportunities. It may be those new relationships or that new career that launches you into something dynamic.

We should never be afraid to function outside a comfort zone, for God will eventually bring us into a new and higher comfort zone. Things may seem challenging and disorientating at first, but we do become accustomed to the new things. When we are prepared to step out of our comfort zone, we find that God was already there! No one climbs steps forever. You will eventually reach the top and experience higher comforts. When I started playing guitar in a band, I struggled with timing and just flowing smoothly with the rest of the musicians. I would feel nervous and uncomfortable whenever we performed on stage. However, after much practice and stage performance with the band, I mastered those areas where I was lacking, the result being that I became comfortable playing more skilfully on a new level than when I first started off.

A baby goes from the comfort of the womb to the comfort of its mother's loving arms; however, the transition from womb to arms can be an uncomfortable period for the baby, and more so for the mother. We should not be troubled or stressed out about an uncomfortable period. It is only a transition period. God will take us from one level of comfort to the next. It only gets better with God. He wants us to go from glory to glory. In other words, God wants our lives to get better. He wants us to use the previous level as a foundation or springboard to new levels.

God is able to comfort us and then use us to comfort others. He works through us. We become His hands and feet, so to speak. *2 Corinthians 1:4* says, *"Who comforts us in all our troubles, so that we can comfort those in any trouble with the comfort we ourselves receive from God"*

(NIV). Many times I have been able to comfort and empathise with people who have lost loved ones. Losing my parents and two of my siblings was devastating, yet each time I felt the love and comfort of God, namely through people He placed alongside me to comfort me through those heart-breaking times. I apply this same comfort to others in similar situations.

Uncomfortable moments or durations will come. We must trust God to help us transition through them. As much as we desire comfort and happiness, we do have to allow periods to mourn a loved one who died or who had some tragedy. Jesus said He came to comfort all who mourn. Mourning is part of the healing or recovery process. Even Abraham mourned when his wife died. *"And Abraham came to mourn for Sarah, and to weep for her" (Genesis 23:2 NKJV)*. We also see Jacob mourning for his son Joseph after believing he was torn to pieces by some wild animal. *"Then Jacob tore his clothes, put on sackcloth on his waist, and mourned for his son many days…. Thus his father wept for him" (Genesis 37:34–35 NKJV)*. Joseph's brothers lied to their father, leading him to believe his beloved son was dead. Jacob sank to the depths of sadness because he truly loved his son and the loss was almost unbearable. It is healthy to let it out instead of keeping in those tears. We have emotions. God gave them to us. Sad things can cause us to be hurt. The key though is to allow God and time to bring healing and comfort so we do not remain in perpetual sorrow. King David spent many days mourning the sickness of one of his children. After the child died, David was able to move on beyond the initial devastating pain of the loss of his child *(2 Samuel 12:18–23)*. Life has to go on. We do not forget our loved ones. When we remember them, we do not hurt as much as before. I still think about my parents and siblings I lost, but the pain of loss is not severe now.

Jesus experienced discomfort for our sake. His crucifixion was a gruesome experience. He went through it so we could experience the joy and comfort of salvation and the promise of Heaven. Our comfort abounds through Christ *(2 Corinthians 1:5)*. While there are many distressingly uncomfortable things in this world, God promised a blessed time for us in Heaven where no discomfort or terror or evil will exist. A place of comfort is one where we are secure, safe, at peace, joyful and satisfied. It sounds like utopia — and indeed it is. Heaven is real and its comforts are real. It is a place where there is total bliss. It is a paradise. There is no sadness, sickness, pain or death. There is only life and blessing. Eden represented Heaven in many aspects until sin destroyed that. God gave Adam three important things in Eden: *Life, Blessing and God-Presence.* This was life without death. Eden was a place without curse, fear and shame.

The apostle Paul admonished believers to comfort one another with the truth that one day Jesus will return to take us home to Heaven to be with Him. This reality ought to comfort our hearts, especially in a world that is becoming hostile in many ways: *"For the Lord Himself will descend from Heaven with a shout, with the voice of an archangel, and with a trumpet of God. And the dead in Christ will rise first. Then we who are alive and remain shall be caught up together with them in the clouds to meet the Lord in the air. And thus we shall always be with the Lord. Therefore comfort one another with these words" (1 Thessalonians 4:16–18 NKJV).*

RECAP

- Certain comforts are good for the soul. God understands comfort and our need for it. The Bible calls Him the God of all comfort.
- It is the Holy Spirit who connects our spirit with God, enabling us to experience intimacy with Him and giving us a sense of belonging. The Spirit lets us know that we are children of God.
- Having the Holy Spirit is God's way of saying to us, *"I will never leave you, nor forsake you" (Hebrews 13:5 NKJV)*. Knowing that God is always with us is very comforting, especially when we face adverse circumstances.
- God the Holy Spirit is our Helper. The Greek word is *paraklétos* ("counsellor, helper, comforter and assistant"). *Klétos* means "called" or "divinely appointed". When *para* and *klétos* are combined we see that the Holy Spirit was divinely appointed or called to be beside us, and He is also in us.
- Some comforts are not sin but can become obstacles if they slow or hinder our growth.
- We should never be afraid to function outside a comfort zone, for God will eventually bring us into a new and higher comfort zone.
- God is able to comfort us and then use us to comfort others.
- Sad things can cause us pain. The key though is to allow God and time to bring healing and comfort so we do not remain in perpetual sorrow.

===================================

"The stars may fall, but God's promises will stand and be fulfilled."

J. I. Packer

===================================

Chapter 8: Promise Keeper

"He who promised is faithful" (Hebrews 10:23 NKJV).

A reassuring and comforting reality about God is that He is constant. He does not change or waver. He is not doubleminded. In addition to that, He is all-powerful. When He gives His Word, it is a sure Word that will come to pass. In fact, God places a high value on His Word *(Psalm 138:2)*. Every word from God shall come to pass. No one, not even the Devil, has the power to negate God's Word and what God purposes *(Isaiah 22:22)*.

God is not playing games with us — He says what He means and means what He says. The wonderful thing about God is that He never breaks His promises. People intend to do things that they sometimes never end up doing. Promises are not intentions. Intentions do not have to be fulfilled, but promises do. If God said it He will do it. In other words, God never fails to honour His Word. He said that His Word will accomplish that which He sends it out to do; it will not return to Him void *(Isaiah 55:11)*. When planted, the Word will become abundantly fruitful. God makes good promises and He fulfils every word of those promises.

Another word for promise is "vow". When I served on the youth leadership team many years ago at Eden Full Gospel Church in South Africa, the youth were encouraged to make a vow to God and their parents that they would remain chaste until the day of marriage. Only those who were serious about it went through with it. Each got a ring that symbolized sexual purity until marriage. This was a huge thing for them, especially because they live in a world where promiscuity is prevalent. Therefore, they were given enough time to think long and hard about making such a vow. It was voluntary, but still a big deal. God Himself cautions us from making vows or promises we have no intention of keeping *(Ecclesiastes 5:4)*.

We are living in a generation where people do not keep their word or promise as they ought to. We find it hard to trust someone who does not value or keep their word. A promise by nature is "yes" and must be fulfilled. We often break our promises for various reasons. Obviously it is understandable if the circumstances overpower our ability to fulfil a promise, but we must deliver when the circumstances permit. This means avoiding unwarranted excuses. We all depend on

God and His ability to fulfil His promises. This makes Him trustworthy and reliable.

No matter what we go through, we have an assurance that GOD WILL BRING US OUT. God does not leave us in the prison or dungeon. He does not leave us in the storm or the desert. He has a better place for us. He promised the Israelites that He would take them to a land where they would not be hunted and overcome by enemies. It would be a place where they would find rest and sustenance. They would be able to live in abundance and comfort. The journey had many ups and downs, but none of that could stop them from getting to where God was taking them. God does not just promise with words, but He has the ability to bring that promise to reality. I would not promise my son an aeroplane because I do not have the ability or means to get him one. However, I have promised him a car one day because I can at least afford that. Whatever God has promised us He can afford. Latin writer Publilius Syrus said these wise words: *"Never promise more than you can perform."* PROMISES MEAN NOTHING IF THEY CANNOT BE FULFILLED!

Our expectation comes from the surety of God's promises. The Jews expected a Messiah because God had promised them one. Abraham and Sarah expected a son even though they were barren because God had promised them one. Manoah's barren wife expected Samson, a great warrior, because God had promised them a son as well. The disciples expected the power of God to show up in the upper room because Jesus had promised the Holy Spirit would come. We expect Jesus to return because He promised us that He will. Being sure of God's promises will lift our expectation.

After four hundred years of slavery we would think that God had completely forgotten his children, but He sent Moses and worked with him to deliver the Israelites *(Exodus 3)*. This was a promise He had made to Abraham even before his descendants could be enslaved. During those four hundred years in slavery, their enemy, Egypt, seemed greater, stronger and intimidating, yet when God got involved, the enslaved Hebrews became stronger than their captors. *Psalm 40: 1–2* says, *"I waited patiently for the Lord; And He inclined to me, And heard my cry. He also brought me up out of a horrible pit, Out of the miry clay, And set my feet upon a rock, And established my steps"* (NKJV).

No matter what situation one may find oneself in, God has a way of changing those situations in a glorious manner. He is able to turn enemies into friends. He is able to unite estranged families. He is able to heal bodies devastated by fatal diseases. God is able to make kings out of shepherd boys and queens out of orphaned girls. The possibilities are endless with God.

The following verse from *1 Kings 8:56* is probably one of the most powerful ones in regard to God's unfailing promises: *"Blessed be the LORD, who has given rest to His people Israel, according to all that He promised. There has not failed one word of all His good promise, which He promised through His servant Moses" (NKJV).* God had promised to deliver Israel from cruel Egyptian bondage, and He did. He promised to protect and care for them even in the wilderness, and did just that by defending them against enemies and feeding them in the wilderness. He enabled Joshua to lead them into the land He had promised their forefathers.

God does not promise calamity for us, but rather immeasurably good things. Persecution and buffeting come from the enemy. I heard author and co-pastor Nicole Crank say, *"God will use the rocks that were meant for your tombstone for your stepping stone."* In other words, the things that were meant to destroy us will become a springboard to catapult us into a great destiny. God knows about our troubles and He is willing to do something about them. Our God is into solutions. When we have trouble, we attract God. He is a present help in time of trouble *(Psalm 46:1).* God raised Moses appropriately for the destiny that was in store for him in the enemy's den, Pharaoh's palace, and then later used the skills which Moses had acquired there to facilitate the deliverance and leading of His people.

God has already seen everyone's whole life. Nothing catches Him by surprise. He knows the end from the beginning *(Isaiah 46:10).* When God was getting ready to deliver the Israelites, He already had a place for them to go. He also took the wealth of the Egyptians and blessed the Israelites with it. He is a good God who has good things for us. He takes us to good places. Moses understood and trusted God when he said, *"I will say of the LORD, 'He is my refuge and my fortress; My God, in Him I will trust'. Surely He will deliver you from the snare of the fowler [enemy] And from the perilous pestilence [deadly diseases]" (Psalm 91:2–3 NKJV).*

What has God promised us? If it has not yet come to pass, we must hold on and keep believing. God is working it out for us. Even if there is total disappointment on the journey, God will use it for our good.

God turns all that the enemy meant for evil around and uses it for our good, and He gets the glory. If we could ask Abraham, he would tell us God keeps His promises. If we could ask Joseph, he would tell us God keeps His promises. God showed Joseph through dreams that he would be prominent. He would be a prolific and sustaining leader. This came to pass even with all the adverse circumstances that came against him.

I look back over my life and reflect on all the good God has done for me. I have seen of all the things He promised to do for and through me come to pass. I think of all the dangers He rescued me from. I think of all the times I felt alone and lost, yet He was right there with me, loving and comforting me. He is a promise-keeper, and He is here to stay. I have no fear of the future because the God I serve owns the future.

When Abraham asked his chief servant to go and find his son a good wife, he made his servant swear that he would do just that *(Genesis 24:2–4)*. When God makes promises to us, He has no one greater than Himself to swear by, so He swears by Himself. *"For when God made a promise to Abraham, because He could swear by no one greater, He swore by Himself, saying, 'Surely blessing I will bless you, and multiplying I will multiply you'" (Hebrews 6:13–14 NKJV)*. From this we can gather that swearing (making promises) is a serious thing.

God's promises may seem delayed, but they are never denied. We must trust His timing. I may have promised my son a car, but he will not get it until he is old and mature enough to handle it. God is a good Father. He knows exactly when to fulfil certain promises in our lives. In His perfect timing He makes all things beautiful. Without His timing and our maturity to handle the promises, they can end by being a burden instead of a blessing.

And as I have mentioned before, here is the biggest promise of all in Scripture that has yet to be fulfilled: Jesus made a promise that He will return for us and take us to Heaven. To prove His seriousness, He gave us the precious Holy Spirit as a down payment or guarantee that He will return. We probably have all bought something on what they call *lay buy or layaway. This simply means the item is being reserved only for you.* After putting down a portion of the payment for a particular item of clothing or furniture, the store holds it for you. No one can buy it or take it. The store is certain you will return for it because you have left something of value behind — your money. When you return a few days, weeks or even months later with the final payment, that item is still there for you. This is the concept God used when He declared that the Holy Spirit is our down payment. The Bible calls Him the Spirit of promise. *Ephesians 1:13* says, *"In Him you also trusted, after you heard the word of truth, the gospel of your salvation; in whom also, having believed, you were sealed with the Holy Spirit of promise, who is the guarantee of our inheritance until the redemption of the purchased possession, to the praise of His glory" (NKJV).* No one can have us. We are the Lord's. He will return for us. That is going to happen. I am excited about that. We will see God, our true Father and life source. Expect it because He promised it.

The best thing we can do for ourselves in a turbulent world is to believe God. Hold on to His promises. God is full of integrity. Everything else will pass away but not the Word of God *(Matthew 5:18)*. *Psalm 119:89* tells us that God's Word is forever settled. When we know and believe God's promises we can live in confidence instead of anxiety.

Our God who made great promises to us is very faithful *(Hebrews 10:23)*. We are encouraged not to waver concerning the promises of God because He is completely dependable and reliable. We are called upon to exercise patience until the end, knowing we will inherit God's promises *(Hebrews 6:12)*. We can expect healing, power, blessing and every other good thing because God promised them to us.

RECAP

- When God gives His Word, it is a sure Word that will come to pass. He places the highest value on His Word *(Psalm 138:2)*.
- God never fails to perform His Word. He said that His Word will accomplish that which He sends it out to do.
- God himself cautions us from making vows or promises we have no intention of keeping.
- God has the ability to bring promises to reality.
- Even if there is total disappointment on the journey, God will use it for our good. All that the enemy meant for evil is turned by God for our good, and He gets the glory.
- We can expect healing, power and all kinds of blessings because God promised us them.
- We are encouraged not to waver concerning the promises of God because He is completely dependable and reliable.
- God's promises may seem delayed, but they are never denied. We must trust His timing.
- Without His timing and our maturity to handle the promises, prematurely answered prayers can end by being a burden instead of a blessing.
- Jesus made a promise that He will return for us and take us to Heaven. He gave us the precious Holy Spirit as a down payment or guarantee that He will return.

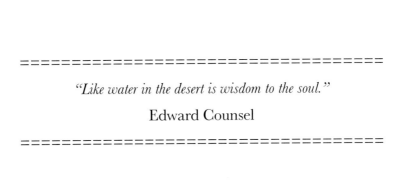

=====================================

"Like water in the desert is wisdom to the soul."

Edward Counsel

=====================================

Chapter 9: Wise Counsellor

Everything God has to say comes with a bucketload of wisdom, and we would do well to pay attention to His instructions. God does not operate with human wisdom. In order to access, activate or operate in this wisdom, one firstly has to believe that God exists *(Hebrews 11:6)*, for His ways and workings are far above what we can imagine or understand. Secondly, God must be trusted because He is God. The great scientist Isaac Newton said, *"This most beautiful system of the sun, planets and comets, could only proceed from the counsel and dominion of an intelligent and powerful Being (God)."* The perfect and well-designed planet could only be the work of our wise and intelligent God.

God appeared in a dream to a man called Solomon who had just become king after his father David passed on. God promised to give Solomon anything he wanted. If that was me, perhaps I would have asked for longer life, a huge mansion or a large amount of finance. What about you? Solomon surprised us all. He asked God for WISDOM. If we do not understand the power and value of wisdom, we will dismiss it as a small thing. But wisdom is the main thing in life *(Proverbs 4:7)*. In fact, wisdom will reward the one who seeks it *(Proverbs 2)*.

God granted King Solomon wisdom on how to handle his position of kingship. For example: A mother, who smothered her baby to death and switched her dead baby with her friend's living one, came before Solomon. Both women now claimed the baby belonged to them. The guilty mother agreed with Solomon that the baby should be cut in half with the a sword so each mother would get half. However, the real mother of the living baby cried out in protest. She told the king to give the baby to the guilty mother. At least her baby would still be alive, even if now reared by the fake mother. Solomon did this to discern who the real mother was. He then ordered that the baby be returned to its rightful mother, who wanted it to live. The fake mother did not care if the baby died, for it was not hers. Such wisdom that Solomon walked in came from God.

We must ask God for wisdom so we can carry out our day-to-day tasks in the best possible way. When we are presented with challenges, we can discern with Godly wisdom which direction to take. No wise person continues to walk in a path that leads to destruction. *"There is a way that seems right to a man, but its end is the way of death" (Proverbs 14:12 NKJV)*. A spider's web seems harmless until the insect gets trapped in it. For example, there are many things that people engage in that seem harmless, but end up causing them great sorrow. Some people have dabbled in the occult or black magic out of fun or curiosity to their own detriment. Some start off gambling for fun but end up heavily addicted and lose large sums of money.

God offers us wisdom freely if we want it *(James 1:5)*. Wisdom helps us combat things that try to pollute our lives. Walking wisely crushes pride, foolishness, ignorance and bitterness. *"Who is wise and understanding among you? Let him show it by good conduct that his works are done in the meekness of wisdom" (James 3:13 NKJV)*. The Bible clearly points out that humility comes from wisdom. Abigail was wise enough to humble herself before King David and apologize for her foolish husband, Nabal who mistreated the king's men. Hence, her life and that of her household was spared, and she became David's wife after her foolish husband lost his life.

People who are full of pride normally do not listen to the advice of others because they think their own advice is better. God offers the best counsel. *"I will instruct you and teach you in the way you should go; I will counsel you with my loving eye on you" (Psalm 32:8, NIV)*. Following God's advice is like encountering a fountain of life. God's wisdom is pure. It makes us peaceful, considerate and submissive to Him. People who operate in pride, hatred, stubbornness and strife are unwise. God offers us His wisdom so we can live good and blessed lives. Wise people always seek out wise counsel, but the unwise do not because they are wise in their own eyes *(Proverbs 26:12)*.

The Bible is not a leisure book. It is a book for life. It is very helpful in every aspect of life. There are answers in it. There are instructions in it for us to follow and benefit from. If we do not apply these wonderful instructions, then we will malfunction. It is like buying a device and not bothering with the manual until a problem is encountered. The Bible is our manual for life. God is our manufacturer, so to speak. He knows exactly how we ought to function. The problem is that many people think they know better than He does. We are the clay (creatures, not self-made) and God is the potter (the Creator). The clay does not tell the potter how it ought to be made or fashioned and what function it will serve. The potter (manufacturer) decides that.

God teaches us to leave our simple ways and walk in His wisdom that leads to paths of righteousness and fulfilment without regret. *"Forsake foolishness and live, And go in the way of understanding" (Proverbs 9:6 NKJV).* God teaches us that when we get to know Him, we receive wisdom *(Proverbs 9:10).*

God says that the love of money can lead people into troubles that bring them grief. *1 Timothy 6:10* says, *"For the love of money is a root of all kinds of evil. Some people, eager for money, have wandered from the faith and pierced themselves with many griefs."* Money itself does not do this, but greed for it. God teaches us that money ought not to be our master, but a tool or servant *(Matthew 6:24).*

God teaches us how to use our tongues wisely. The tongue, being a small member of the body, can set the world on fire *(James 3:5).* The tongue is like a small rudder that directs the path of the large ship. We eat the fruit of our own lips *(Proverbs 12:14).* What is happening in your life? If you do not like it, check what you have been continually confessing and believing. Wise words have benefits. We have to deal with the heart. When the heart is right, the mouth will speak well. Usually the mouth just gives voice to what is in the heart. Out of the heart flow the issues of life.

God teaches us how to maintain healthy relationships. We are encouraged to forgive and show compassion towards each other *(Colossians 3:13).* We are encouraged to help others and be concerned with their lives, not just our own *(Philippians 2:3).* God's Word cautions us to build trust and not betray the confidence of our friends or spouses. We are encouraged to inspire others to do good. It makes the world a better place.

God teaches parents to impart wisdom to their children. As a parent, I do not want to walk in wisdom while my children walk in foolishness and bring trouble on themselves. No parent wants to build their family or business or ministry with wisdom and success, only to have it all torn down through the foolishness of their successors. Leaders must impart wisdom to those under them. It is not just about passing on the baton, but also wisdom on how to handle it. Can the next leader handle the responsibilities and functioning of the business, ministry or empire with wisdom? King Solomon said, *"Then I hated all my labour in which I had toiled under the sun, because I must leave it to the man who will come after me. And who knows whether he will be wise or a fool? Yet he will rule over all my labour in which I toiled and in which I have shown myself wise under the sun" (Ecclesiastes 2:18–19 NKJV).*

God teaches a young man to stay away from the adulterous woman, the woman who seems beautiful and enticing but will end up leading him into sin and destruction. *"For the lips of an immoral woman drip honey, and her mouth is smoother than oil; But in the end she is bitter as wormwood, Sharp as a two edged sword. Her feet go down to death, Her feet lay hold of hell" (Proverbs 5:3–5 NKJV).* This warning applies to young girls, too, to stay away from guys who want only to use them for selfish gain. In other words, apply wisdom when seeking relationships. Find a spouse who will add value and strength to your life. *Proverbs 5:18–20* says, *"Enjoy the wife you married as a young man! Lovely as an angel, beautiful as a rose — don't ever quit taking delight in her body. Never take her love for granted! Why would you trade enduring intimacies for cheap thrills with a whore? For dalliance [a casual sexual relationship] with a promiscuous stranger?" (MSG).* Men are encouraged to find that *Proverbs 31* woman. She does her husband good. She is industrious. She cares for her family. She is not lazy but works with willing hands. She sees to the day-to-day tasks that lead to the effective and efficient running of the home. She assists her husband. She has Godly counsel on her lips. Her children and husband praise her.

There are many things that my parents instructed me in that have benefited my life greatly. For example: they taught me to be honest and not to steal; they taught me to be polite and to work hard. They taught me to finish whatever I started. I am glad I listened and acted upon those wise instructions. Then I think of all the ones I did not follow and how I suffered for them. For example: I allowed a friend to copy my answers during a test at school. Both he and I got into trouble and ended up in school detention. We must not be wise in our own eyes. We must stay humble, for it enables us to learn from those wiser than we are.

Being omniscient, God knows much more than we do. His counsel over our lives is for our benefit. He considers all aspects of our lives. People, in their limited wisdom, can cause us to follow an instruction that ends up putting some other area of our lives out of joint, so to speak. When God instructs us in one area, it does not harm other areas of our lives. God has a holistic approach when dealing with us.

No one can serve two masters. We have to choose. Will a person serve their own human wisdom or will they depend on God's wisdom? Will a person choose their own way or God's way? What have they learned from their mistakes? Better still, how can they avoid making those mistakes by learning from the mistakes of others? We are not perfect. We do make mistakes. We get things wrong, but those wrong things can be corrected, if we are willing to change.

Solomon is known as the wisest man who ever lived, but there came a time when he started to ignore God's wise counsel and listened to the plea of his heathen wives to allow worship of false gods. They turned his heart away from God. The wise and understanding heart God had given Solomon was now darkened by ungodly ways. Even after God urged him to turn away from false gods and repent, he refused. The results were sad. Because of this the kingdom was divided and Israel faced many troubles *(1 Kings 11:11)*.

After Solomon died, his idiotic son Rehoboam became king. Rehoboam lacked good judgement when he took on board the ill advice of his personal advisers to make things harder for the people under him. He lost the people's support and they sought another ruler. It is important whose advice we accept. Foolish advice yields foolish results.

God's counsel is not burdensome. There is life and liberty in His commands. The burdens come from following our own foolish ways. If we refuse to bend our choices to the will of God, then His will cannot work perfectly in our lives. It is a partnership. God does his part and we ought to do ours. We are the students and God is the Master. People who insist on being masters of their own destiny end up making a mess of their lives. We are better off allowing God to influence our choices with His wisdom.

When things go wrong people are prone to blame God. On close examination they realize it was because of their own lack of Godly counsel. Job blamed God for all of the catastrophic events in his life. God challenged him in the end. God said, *"Who is this that darkens my counsel with words without knowledge" (Job 38:2 NKJV)*. Job himself placed his hand over his mouth and said, *"I put my hand over my mouth" (Job 40:4)*. God cannot be corrected. He has never been wrong, and never will be.

When I was twelve years old, I used to help my father every time he worked on his car. My father was very skilled with his hands as well as his brain. There were a lot of things that he did with his hands and he did a marvellous job with them. Much of that rubbed off on me and some of my siblings. We were skilled at multiple things. We found it easy to pick up skills with minimum training. We just had a knack for certain things, whether it was mechanical, carpentry, fencing, painting or agriculture. I learned many things from my parents. Today I still put some of those skills to use. However, at thirteen I wanted to drive my father's car. He told me I was too young and did not know how to drive. I kept pestering him to no end, so one Sunday afternoon he handed me the keys and allowed me to manoeuvre the car in our wide yard. I grabbed the keys without even stopping to ask for some instructions. I slipped into the driver's seat with glee as my older brother got in the passenger's side. It was an automatic Chevrolet. I fired up the engine, placed my foot on the gas pedal and selected R for reverse. The car shot back so suddenly and forcefully that both I and my brother screamed out of fear.

Two of my other siblings who were milling around idly watching my first driving experience quickly scattered away, yelling to my father to come to the rescue. I am not sure how the car stopped but I am glad it did. My father emerged from the house, a slight smile on his face. I think he was more amused than shocked or annoyed. My brother got out as quickly as he could and left me in the car. Driving did not seem like fun, after all. My father opened the door on the driver's side and told me to scoot over to the passenger's seat. He then told me to listen carefully and watch what he did. He started the car, placed his right foot on the brake pedal and then selected reverse. He then put down the handbrake and slowly lifted his foot from the brake. The car started to move backwards gently. He reapplied pressure on the brake and the car stopped. He then selected drive and slowly released the brake and the car moved forward. It all made sense. Was I eager to retry? No! But I knew what was coming. *"Would you like to try again?"* he asked. I did, and it all went smoothly as I followed his leading to a T. We did it a few times until I was smiling again. After the third time, my father said, *"That's good, you've got it."* I climbed out of the car, shoulders broad, head held high, feeling proud that I could move the car. I know it was just back and forth, but still, at thirteen, that was thrilling for me. By the age of seventeen I was pretty much a skilled driver.

There are many things in life that excite us. We tend to rush off to do them without taking time to think things through. Instead of enjoying the experiences we end up regretting them because we failed to listen and learn and pay attention. Taking time to listen and learn before the execution of something can save us unnecessary disappointment. Let us take time to consider God's wise counsel. We raise our level of understanding and living with His counsel.

RECAP

- Everything God has to say comes with a bucketload of wisdom. We should to pay attention to His instructions.
- Wisdom is the principal key for successful living *(Proverbs 4:7)*. In fact, wisdom will reward the one who seeks it *(Proverbs 2)*.
- When we are presented with challenges, we can discern with Godly wisdom which direction to take.
- Wise people always seek out wise counsel, but the unwise do not, for they are wise in their own eyes *(Proverbs 26:12)*.
- Leaders must pass the baton on to those under them, and impart wisdom on how to handle it.
- God teaches us to leave our simple ways and walk in His wisdom that leads to paths of righteousness and fulfilment without regret.
- Our omniscient God knows much more than we do. He counsels us for our benefit, carefully considering every aspect of our lives.
- God's counsel is not burdensome. There is life and liberty in His commands. Burdens come when we follow our own foolish ways.
- Take time to consider God's wise counsel. Taking heed of His counsel raises our level of understanding and the quality of our lives.

====================================
"I believe that every human mind feels pleasure in doing good to another."
Thomas Jefferson
====================================

Chapter 10: Presence and Pleasure

"In the presence of the Lord there is fullness of joy and at His right hand pleasures evermore" (Psalm 16:11 NKJV).

Godly pleasure has a source — GOD. Pleasure in its purest sense is very beneficial in our lives. The Bible bears witness that God does a lot of things for His good pleasure. God has pleasure only in what is upright *(1 Chronicles 29:17)*. We love pleasure because God does too, and we are made in His image and likeness.

Unfortunately, the word "pleasure" often gets associated with sin and debauchery; after all, people frequently indulge in acts that are very pleasurable but sinful or harmful. The Bible calls such indulgences *"worldly pleasures" (Titus 2:12)*. Other words associated with this are "lust" and "perversion". Drug addiction may be pleasurable for a season or moment but can cause serious harm. Promiscuity (sex outside of marriage with multiple partners) is a misguided pleasure that carries the risk of contracting deadly diseases, and of course, violates God's statutes on sexual matters. Gossiping may seem enjoyable, but when one ends up losing good friends over it, that joy turns to regret and mistrust.

Gratification is a human need that God designed us to have, which comes in many ways: it can be derived from food, sex, recreation, purpose and other things. Food is designed to keep us alive physically, but God gave us taste buds so we could enjoy our food. Procreation allows for population. God gave men and women the ability to procreate, and with that comes great pleasure. There is a long list of things that we engage in with pleasure attached to them. When we enjoy the company of friends, we have God to thank for that. When a mother or father holds their baby in their arms and feel that great love for them that brings joy, they have God to thank for the ability to create and love. I believe God wants us to have fun. His gifts ought to bring joy. Personally, I derive great pleasure watching my children enjoy their toys and gadgets. God does not give us gifts so we can be miserable.

Most things we do bring pleasure in some way, whether immediately or sometime later. Even when I work out at the gym, I find pleasure in knowing I am keeping my body fit and developing my muscles, though there is certain amount of pain that goes with it. Long hours of study may seem devoid of pleasure, but when you receive those outstanding results and awards, pleasure is surely there. Obviously, there are things that are worth waiting for. Everything has a time and season. For example, most fruits can be thoroughly enjoyed only when they are ripe or mature. If an immediate gratification is going to cause you future pain, it would be wise to abstain or wait for the right time.

Jesus Himself found pleasure in going to the cross. Do not misunderstand me, He knew He was going to endure gruesome suffering during His crucifixion, but the joy was in what that cross experience would accomplish for us. *"He was willing to die a shameful death on the cross because of the joy he knew would be His afterwards; and now He sits in the place of honour by the throne of God" (Hebrews 12:2, TLB).*

God does not just keep pleasure to Himself, but hands it out to us. He wants us to experience the pleasures He has for us. *Psalm 16:11* says, *"You have let me experience the joys of life and the exquisite [lovely] pleasures of Your eternal presence" (TLB).* The New King James version expresses it this way: *"In Your presence is fullness of joy; At Your right hand pleasures forevermore."* God has lasting pleasures with no sorrow added. God's blessings are not like pills that come with unpleasant side effects.

God created us for His own good pleasure. He takes pleasure in us *(Psalm 149:4)* and also wants us to live in His pleasure. Adam was created in God's presence. God breathed into his nostrils and Adam became a living soul *(Genesis 2:7)*. God formed Adam and breathed him into existence personally. We exist by the breath or Spirit of God. We are alive because He is alive. A dead God cannot produce life. Our God is NOT DEAD, but He is ALIVE. In Eden, Adam had every blessing and the awesome presence of God. God has been working to bring us back into His presence since Adam and Eve were banished from Eden and from His wonderful manifested presence. Like an orphan, Cain left the presence of God and became a wanderer due to his own evil actions.

God does not want to leave us like orphans. Because of Jesus, God has become our Abba Father: *"For you have not received the spirit of bondage again to fear, but you have received the Spirit of adoption by whom we cry out, Abba Father. The Spirit Himself bears witness with our spirit, that we are the children of God" (Romans 8:15–16 NKJV).* As children of God, we will never be orphaned again. We are always accepted in our Father's presence. He identifies with us.

God is pleasant company. I don't know about you, but I am a *presence-addict*. I love God's divine presence: I feel balance, equilibrium, synergy, power and wholeness there. His presence is comforting, restorative and peaceful. You can rest there. Many times I have entered God's presence troubled by various things, but only to feel all those anxieties melt away in His presence and be replaced by a peace, joy and contentment that passes all understanding. I also know of people who have experienced physical and emotional healing just from worshipping God and abiding in His divine presence.

When Adam and Eve sinned, God did not communicate intimately and freely with them in the same way He did before, yet He did not entirely abandon them. He remained involved in their lives. When I decided to covenant with God at the age of nineteen, I was under the impression that God started helping me only then. It was quite the opposite. God was the one who sent other believers into my life to redirect my life. He had a plan for my life long before I realized who He was. God was patient with me, not willing that I should perish.

God has been working patiently with mankind. Whenever He found a man or woman who was willing to follow Him, He revealed Himself in greater measure to them. He revealed Himself to Noah, whereby He preserved him and his family in the Ark during the great Flood *(Genesis 6)*. The name "Noah" has two meanings. The first meaning is "wandering". Before God showed up in His life Noah was wandering or living without hope in an evil generation who had no regard for God. The Bible says their hearts were continually wicked. But Noah found grace in the eyes of God *(Genesis 6:5–8)*. After destroying every living thing except Noah and his family and selected creatures, God started again. It was not God's initial intention to wipe out creation, yet it was not in God's nature to allow evil to escalate and be rampant on earth. The world we live in now will come under judgement, but those of us who are in Christ have passed from judgement to life and reward *(John 5:24)*.

The second meaning of Noah's name is "rest". When Noah encountered God, he came into rest. He came into safety and a God-directed life. There is something about God's presence that makes us feel restful and safe. God kept Noah and his family safe in the Ark and kept up a relationship with them after the Flood.

Another man God worked through was Abraham, whom I mentioned earlier, in chapter 4. Then God worked through Isaac and Jacob. He also worked through Joseph, Miriam, Moses and Aaron as well as King David. He worked through the prophets, such as Elijah and Isaiah. He worked through John the Baptist and the apostles in the New Testament. He is working through us believers too. God wants to invade every heart with His love and presence.

God intended not to be far from creation but to be near. The Bible describes a time when God would come down and talk with Moses. It must have been glorious. *Exodus 33:10–11* says, *"All the people saw the pillar of cloud standing at the tabernacle door, and all the people rose and worshipped, each man in his tent. So the LORD spoke to Moses face to face, as a man speaks to his friend" (NKJV).* Moses grew to love the presence of God. Moses spent forty days and forty nights in the manifested presence of the Lord on Mount Sinai. Sinai means "pointed". We cannot reach the highest points or places in our lives without God. Mount Sinai is also known as Mount Horeb, the "holy place". God directed Moses to meet Him there *(Exodus 34:2)*. When we meet or encounter God, He draws us higher up. We experience elevation in every area of our lives. Mount Sinai is also the "place of revelation". Moses received the Ten Commandments there. We receive revelation when we are in God's manifested presence. There are times in worship, when God gives me words of knowledge and prophetic messages for the church, or for individuals.

Moses neither ate nor drank anything for forty days and nights while in God's presence. God preserved him. In fact, Moses came out looking and feeling better after being in God's presence. His skin shone brightly — so much so, in fact, that the people were afraid to come near him, causing him to don a veil when speaking to them *(Exodus 34:29–35)*. They could not handle the residue of God's glory on Moses's face. Sometime later, this glorious light would fade from Moses's face, but the Bible tells us that there is coming a day when God's glory on us will never fade, for we will be in His presence continually. We will have glorified bodies that will be able to handle the greater weight of His glory. Jesus, who removed the veil through His crucifixion, has not only unveiled the glory of God to us, but also unveiled our hearts to see and believe *(2 Corinthians 3:13–17)*.

There is something wonderful about the presence of God that causes us to fall on our knees and worship. He lifts every heavy weight. When Paul and Silas were in prison, they began praising God at midnight. The Bible tells us that God invaded that prison and broke their chains off *(Acts 16:23–28)*. Not only did the chains fall off Paul and Silas, but also off all the other prisoners. Your deliverance will affect others around you. In God's presence, yokes break and bondages are loosened.

In the Old Testament, the high priest would enter the holy of holies to atone for the sins of the people *(Leviticus 16)*. He did so only after presenting a sacrifice for himself and going through a cleansing ritual. If protocol was not followed as God stipulated, that high priest dropped dead in the holy of holies. Thank God this all changed with the inception of the new covenant Jesus made through His shed blood.

When Jesus died on the cross, the curtain in the temple was torn from top to bottom *(Luke 23:45)*. God Himself tore it. He did it to let us know that the dividing wall or curtain was now demolished between Him and us. Through the sin-cleansing blood of Jesus, we now have access to the Father without the fear of perishing in His presence. Jesus came to unveil the Father. Now we receive power, revelation and acceptance in His presence. The removing of the veil allows us to behold God in the beauty of His holiness. I cannot wait for that face-to-face meeting with my Father! Jesus did not just enter the Heavenly tabernacle alone, but granted us access too, as seen when the unknown author of Hebrews writes: *"Therefore, brothers and sisters, since we have confidence to enter the Most Holy Place by the blood of Jesus, by a new and living way opened for us through the curtain, that is his body, and since we have a great priest [Jesus] over the house of God, let us draw near to God with a sincere heart and with full assurance"* (Hebrews 10:19–21, NIV).

It is quite interesting to note that God did not build a building and place His presence in it when He first created the earth. He placed His Spirit or presence in mankind. After man was separated from God by sin, He made His presence manifest in the tabernacle *(Exodus 25:21–22)*. In Genesis, God came to man, and even after the Fall, God still reached out to mankind, but primarily through the priests and prophets. The holy of holies was off limits.

God never intended to dwell in buildings, but meant to dwell in us. God made the temple glorious. However, we are the temple of the Lord. Without His presence, it was just a dead building. We were dead in our spirits without God. Now we are alive because He lives in us by the power and presence of the Holy Spirit. God makes us glorious. We are spiritually alive (reborn and reconnected) because of Him. Instead of now residing in a building made by human hands, God took up residence in us, buildings made by His hands. *"We are the temple of the living God" (2 Corinthians 6:16, NIV)*.

Moses depended on God's presence. He refused to go anywhere without God. *"If Your Presence does not go with us, do not bring us up from here" (Exodus 33:15 NKJV)*. I love what God said to Moses: *"I know you by name" (Exodus 33:17 NKJV)*. This speaks of intimacy and closeness. This shows that God is interested in us. We are not like some manufactured object on an assembly line with a batch number no one cares about. God knows every detail about our lives. We matter to Him more than we realize.

God's presence is a safe and confident place to be in. God can make us feel safe and brave in the midst of trouble or danger. We do not need the absence of fear to experience safety, but the presence of God, which overwhelms us with His love. This is the love that drives fear away. Even when we cannot feel God's presence, we must rest on the fact that He is there. God wants us to be at ease in His presence, not anxious or nervous. People who are unpredictable or volatile make us nervous when we are in close proximity to them. This is because we are not sure what they will do next. God does not change His character and neither does He break His promises. He promised to love and care for us. In His presence we can receive only good because God is good.

Many people chase various things trying to find that one gratifying and rewarding thing. The best thing we can do for ourselves is to cultivate an atmosphere of daily worship in God's presence. We ought to be presence-seekers more than seekers of material things. Material things cannot produce the presence of God, but the presence of God can produce material things. Because of God's power and presence, Isaac reaped a hundredfold harvest from sowing in a barren land where drought was rife at the time *(Genesis 26:1–3,12–14)*. God sustained the Israelites for forty years in the desert by miraculously providing manna and quail. They did not have to keep spare manna for the next day. Each day God sent fresh manna *(Exodus 16)*. Anything kept rotted overnight and was inedible. This tells us that God's presence always produces freshness. He is not doing old things but new things. We must come into God's presence looking for the new, not the old.

While up a high mountain, Jesus changed into a glorious state, brighter than the sun. There appeared Elijah and Moses, also in a glorified state *(Matthew 17:1–5)*. This must have been an amazing sight for the three disciples, Peter, James and John. It was so good, that Peter wanted to build tents or tabernacles for them and just stay up there. We must move beyond simply knowing God and desire also to experience His presence. When we are in God's glorious presence, we want for nothing.

Jesus was rejected on the cross so we would be accepted into God's presence. No child desires an absent father. They need his love and affection and leadership. They need his presence. Mankind does not do well without God. Children do not need just instruction from their father, but his loving touch too. Intimacy with our Heavenly Father is wholesome for our lives.

RECAP

- God does a lot of things for His good pleasure. He has pleasure only in what is upright *(1 Chronicles 29:17)*, and we love it because God does and we are made in His image and likeness.
- Everything has a time and season. If immediate gratification is going to cause you future pain, then abstain.
- God does not only take pleasure in us but also wants us to live in His pleasure.
- God has been working to bring us back into His presence since Adam and Eve were banished from Eden and from His wonderful manifested presence.
- Mount Sanai is also the place of revelation. Moses received the Ten Commandments there. When we are in God's manifested presence, we receive revelation too.
- Instead of now residing in a building made by human hands, God took up residence in us, buildings made by His hands: *"We are the temple of the living God" (2 Corinthians 6:16 NKJV)*.
- We ought to be presence-seekers more than possession-seekers. Material, transient things cannot produce the presence of God, but in the presence of God material things can be produced.
- There is always fresh manna in God's presence. There are new encounters there, not old.
- When we are in God's powerful manifested presence, fear melts away. We want for nothing.

==

"How completely satisfying to turn from our limitations to a God who has none."

A.W. Tozer

==

Chapter 11: Wholesome and Satisfying

God is wholesome and satisfying to the soul of mankind. This is part of that perfect goodness in Him. Wherever God shows up, He brings peace, love, wholeness, satisfaction, providence, joy, freedom and light. People who reject God end up groping in darkness — and I am not talking about physical darkness.

There is a void in every heart that only God can fill. That void comes from a spirit that is dead towards God, one that has not been regenerated. Worldly pleasures and great feats will not fill the void. God wants to be a part of our lives. No man can live unto himself and be thoroughly successful. There is something that every person needs. It is rest for the soul. Putting your tired body down at night and falling into a deep peaceful sleep is satisfying and does wonders for the body and mind. Think of the soul and how it longs for the kind of rest that only God can give it. One really starts living when God takes over one's soul.

Everyone is searching for that one thing that can fill the void in their soul. Look no further than God. Each soul was designed to be satisfied by Him. Nothing but praise will rise from a soul that finds its sustenance in God. King David said, *"My soul shall be satisfied as with marrow and fatness. And my mouth shall praise You with joyful lips" (Psalm 63:5 NKJV).* I love how the Expanded Bible expresses the first line of this verse: *"I will be content as if I had eaten the best foods".* God has the best food for the soul.

Being overly concerned about issues of life weighs us down. Worry and anxiety are not good for the soul. That is why the Bible tells us to be anxious for nothing *(Philippians 4:6).* Worry is like a rocking chair; it cannot take us anywhere. Worry and stress can trigger many health problems, such as high blood pressure, heart disease, diabetes and even obesity. Worry and stress can also affect one's emotions and behaviour.

God instructs us in His Word on what to do or not do. This is to help us navigate successfully through life. He wants to do us good and He wants the best for us, because He is good. God said, *"And I will satiate [fill or satisfy] the soul of the priests with abundance, And My people shall be satisfied with My goodness, says the LORD" (Jeremiah 31:14 NKJV).* God protected Israel, so they would not have to live in fear of being attacked. He provided food and water so they would not have to worry about these basic necessities.

God sent Moses into Egypt to be a deliverer for His people, the Israelites, who were crying out for help because of their hard taskmasters. God is aware of all the trials and tribulations we face in life. He said to Moses, *"I have surely seen the affliction of My people who are in Egypt, and have heard their cry ... for I know their sorrows. So I have come down to deliver them out of the hand of the Egyptians ..." (Exodus 3:7–8 NKJV).* Then God told Moses that He desired to bring His people to a land full of provision where they would be free, blessed and safe. God gave them back their right to freedom, prosperity, safety and dignity. Dignity matters to a person's soul.

Jesus said, *"Come to me, all you who labour and are heavy laden, and I will give you rest. Take My yoke upon you and learn from Me, for I am gentle and lowly in heart, and you will find rest for your souls. For my yoke is easy and My burden is light" (Matthew 11:28 NKJV).* God did not create us to be burdened by the cares of this world. Rather, He created us to dominate and reign through Christ Jesus our Lord. It is easier for the body to be healed and restored than it is for the soul. How many people walk around looking fine externally, but are broken internally? They are bruised in their soul. If only they would realize that there is a soul-healer. His name is Jesus. He is the mender of broken hearts. *Psalm 34:18* says, *"The Lord is close to those whose hearts are breaking; he rescues those who are humbly sorry for their sins" (TLB). Psalm 147:3* says, *"He heals the brokenhearted, binding up their wounds" (TLB).*

Jesus said something very notable and paramount: *"It is written, 'Man shall not live by bread alone, but by every word that proceeds from the mouth of God'" (Matthew 4:4 NKJV).* God nourishes us through our spirits, which has an outworking into our souls and then our bodies. In other words, physical satisfaction cannot make up for soul-satisfaction. The soul has to be fed by God. A soul unfed by God will experience instability and lack. There is a thirst in the soul that only God can adequately satisfy. King David said, *"O God, You are my God; Early will I seek You; My soul thirsts for You; My flesh longs for You" (Psalm 63:1 NKJV).* There are many people who are not completely restful, peaceful and truly content because they have left God out of the equation.

2

Bestselling author and senior pastor John Ortberg wrote, *"You were made for soul-satisfaction, but you will only ever find it in God. The soul craves to be secure. The soul craves to be loved. The soul craves to be significant, and we find these only in God in a form that can satisfy us."*

Man became a living soul after God breathed life into him. Therefore, God is man's true source and satisfier. There are physical things God put on the planet to meet our physical needs. Then there are things that only He can meet in our lives. Knowing the difference and adhering to it will bring balance to our lives. God wants us satisfied, but not apart from Him. He wants us satisfied, but not at the expense of starving or harming other areas of our lives. Therefore, He wants the whole person satisfied. This is why the Bible says, *"The Blessing of the Lord makes one rich, And adds no sorrow with it"* (Proverbs 10:22 NKJV).

A wholesome life starts by understanding and then experiencing God's amazing love and providence. David said that love is better than life itself *(Psalm 63:3)*. God's unfathomable and overwhelming love makes living worthwhile, and makes us feel whole and accepted and cherished. God's love is healthy for the soul in ways we cannot even begin to comprehend.

Love builds and protects the soul. Hate and oppression break it down. Has your soul taken a beating? Is your soul weary? Do you feel violated or stepped on in some way by others? Well, it is time for soul-healing. Satisfaction in the soul cannot be achieved when one clings to offences, regrets and hurts. Do not let old scars remind you of pain but of healing. Do not relive the painful experience; rather, live in the healing. Let your soul rest.

Grateful people experience more satisfaction than those who grumble through life. People who think that the world or God owes them lumber through life with a chip on their shoulder and a less than savoury attitude. We must have an attitude of gratitude. No one can really be content and satisfied with a sour attitude towards life and towards God. We must recognize that God has done so much good for us. We can at least thank Him for that. As a parent, it does my heart good when my children express gratitude for the many things my wife and I do for them. Their gratefulness opens the door even wider for me to do more.

While bringing petitions to God in prayer is right, however, we must not forget to bring Him our praise, too. Speaking on gratitude in his book, *Soul Keeping*, John Ortberg said, *"The Hebrew benedictions (blessings) connected the gift with the Giver. It reminded the citizens of Israel that all that was good came from God. They were training for gratitude, and they loved doing this because they knew life with God was the good life."* By keeping God and all His goodness in mind, we will find more contentment in life.

If I give you a gift and you do not receive it, you will not benefit from it. To benefit from God, we have to receive what He offers. The woman at the well was there to draw natural water. Jesus offered her water that would quench the longing and dryness of her soul. It was an offer, but she had to receive it. Jesus said, *"Whoever drinks of this water will thirst again, but whoever drinks of the water that I shall give him will never thirst. But the water that I shall give him will become in him a fountain of water springing up into everlasting life" (John 4:13–14 NKJV)*. The woman said to Jesus, *"Sir, give me this water, that I may not thirst, nor come here to draw" (John 4:15 NKJV)*. Perhaps she did not quite fully understand the kind of water Jesus was referring to, but she had good sense to ask for it. Jesus was offering her life in her spirit that would permeate her soul and body. It would satisfy her more than the people and things she had been chasing after.

One of the reasons why I love worship is because it puts me in a position where I lift up thanks, praise and adoration to God. It focuses my thoughts on His goodness and less on my problems. We often complain about the negative things in our lives and what we see in the world. However, we have consciously and purposefully to reflect on all the good things that God has done, and in doing so encourage ourselves that He'll do them again, and surpass Himself, if need be. If not, we will be overwhelmed by the negatives, which lead to discouragement and depression. Too much complaining will diminish our gratitude, thereby diminishing the peace our soul needs.

It is not so much the big things that excite me. I wake up and feel that joy of being given another day. I smell that wonderful coffee my wife makes for me and feel grateful. I see my children and feel blessed with such gifts. I look at my wife and how sweet and wonderful and faithful she is and know full well I have been blessed. I think of all the dangers God brought me through and feel so thankful within. I lay my head down at night for a peaceful sleep and thank God for it. All my bodily functions work well. I have more to be thankful for than to complain about. God loves a grateful heart. When my children show gratitude, even for the little things, they set themselves up to receive greater things. Let us practise being more grateful and get to experience greater things in God.

If we met with someone regularly, and all they did was complain, the meeting would become undesirable. Do not get me wrong, God is big enough to handle our complaints, but He would rather have us praise more than complain. He would rather have us be thankful more than discontented. The Bible says that we must make our requests known to God along with thanksgiving *(Philippians 4:6)*. If all we see are the negatives, then praise and gratitude become difficult. Trust me, I can complain at times. Then my wife has to remind me about my Christian commitment to praise and optimism. In case you think I am more of a complainer, let me assure you, I am not. Actually, I am quite an optimistic guy. I look for the light in every dark situation. But even optimists can get a bad dose of despondency at times.

Could anyone possibly see and appreciate God's goodness with constant complaining and a negative outlook on life? I hardly think so. God did not call us to be staunch complainers, but staunch in praise and gratitude. Remember, we give off an atmosphere with whatever flows out of us. God wants us to live in an atmosphere of love, joy, peace and contentment. However, being content does not mean we do not desire more or better. While we reach for more we remain at peace. If the only peace one has is from acquiring material things, then one is in trouble. Nothing can quench the longing of the soul but God. The soul does not need stuff — it needs God.

We tend to want what we see, be it a new house, new car, new mobile phone or other material things. The problem with the eyes is they are never satisfied, so we have to find contentment in what we have. If all a person lives for are material things, then they end up living a shallow life. We get more out of life with God than without Him. Money can buy a bed, but it cannot buy sleep. Money can buy a chair, but it cannot buy a person rest. Money can buy a house, but it cannot make a home or family, and money certainly cannot buy peace for the soul.

One of the many things that vexes people in their soul is fear. God does not want us to fear. *"For God has not given us a spirit of fear, but of power and love and of a sound [stable] mind" (2 Timothy 1:7 NKJV)*. Fear can have a paralyzing effect on people and hinder their progress or ability to take on challenges. King David, who faced many challenges and enemies, said, *"The LORD is my light and my salvation; Whom shall I fear? The LORD is the strength of my life; Of whom shall I be afraid" (Psalm 27:1 NKJV)*. David faced and slew the giant Goliath because he had his focus on God and not on fear or the giant he faced.

Jesus is the great physician who heals the souls of men and women. He provides healing, not just for the physical body but for the soul as well. He wants to bring the hurting to Bethesda, the "House of Grace". Here they do not have to work or sweat to be well, but just receive healing as a gift from Jesus. This reminds me of the words of *Amazing Grace*: *"Amazing grace, how sweet the sound that saved a wretch like me."* This grace cannot be earned. It is a gift.

Satan's goal is to make us think we are alone and do not have help. He wants us to focus on our need, our lack, our brokenness. God wants us to look to Him. He does not want us to pretend or mask the reality of our brokenness but present it to Him. After we present our brokenness to Jesus, we must believe that He will provide our healing. One of the primary things Jesus did on earth was to heal people. He healed the lame, cast out tormenting spirits, raised the dead and rescued others from shameful situations. The shepherd goes after the lost sheep. When he finds it, he carries it back to the fold. Jesus knows where to find us when we are lost or entangled in soul-piercing issues. We must allow Jesus to carry us back to the fold. Like sheep are content in the presence of the shepherd, we ought to be content in Jesus' presence, for He is our chief shepherd.

RECAP

- There is something that every person needs. It is rest for the soul.

- Everyone is searching for that one thing that can fill the void in their soul. Look no further than God. Each soul was designed to be satisfied by Him.

- Jesus said, *"Come to Me, all you who labour and are heavy laden, and I will give you rest. Take My yoke upon you and learn from Me, for I am gentle and lowly in heart, and you will find rest for your souls. For My yoke is easy and My burden is light" (Matthew 11:28 NKJV)*. God did not create us to be burdened by the cares of this world.

- God's love is healthy for the soul in ways we cannot even begin to comprehend. Love builds and protects the soul. Hate and oppression break it down.

- We must have an attitude of gratitude. No one can really be content and satisfied with a sour attitude towards life and towards God. We must recognize that God has done so many good things for us.

- To benefit from God, we have to receive what He offers. The woman at the well was there to draw natural water. Jesus offered her water that would quench the longing and dryness of her soul. It was an offer, but she had to receive it.

- Nothing can quench the longing of the soul but God. The soul does not need stuff — it needs God.

===================================

"Life should not only be lived, it should be celebrated."

Osho

===================================

Chapter 12: Sit Down and Celebrate

My father was a hardworking man, but every time he finished a hard day's work, he would sit down and relax in his favourite sofa without a care in the world. He was restful, happy, satisfied, undisturbed. He was so at ease that you would think he was a lazy man. He found that perfect balance between work and rest. Many people are so busy, they have forgotten what real rest is.

Holidays excite us. It is the thrill of seeing a new place, having a time to kick back and relax, a time for pleasure and recreation. It provides a break in the routine of our day-to-day life of labouring. If a person returns from holiday still stressed and tired, then I question the nature of that holiday. We ought to return happy and rejuvenated.

Physical rest is one thing, but mental rest is quite another. It is hard to get a good night's sleep with a busy or anxious mind. Worry makes people restless. There are times when we just need to sit down and rest, recuperate and even celebrate. God is definitely in favour of this.

God created the earth in six days and then rested on the seventh *(Genesis 2:2)*, not because He was tired, but because He had finished creating. When God finishes something, He takes a seat. He took six days and worked on creating a beautiful earth and every living creature. At the end of that work, He declared Day Seven as a day of rest or celebration. Jesus did the very same thing after His crucifixion, resurrection and ascension; He took a seat besides God the Father. By setting the seventh day aside as a day of rest, God was setting a pattern for us to follow. Work is good with intermittent rest. Taking time aside to rest and to gather around family and friends reminds us that people and relationships are more important than the jobs we have. It allows us to reflect on the goodness of God. When God gave the Israelites the Ten Commandments, He included the sabbath as a day of rest. Interestingly, God instructed them to celebrate their sabbath *(Leviticus 23:32)*. God knows this is good for us. If we do not rest, we will become stressed and burn out because long hours and days of work can starve relationships.

Jesus had a busy ministry that included healing, teaching, training and guiding people. But there were times when He would disappear from the crowds, and even from His disciples to spend time alone

119

with Father God. He would take time away to pray, and I believe He also just found rest and joy basking in the presence of His Father, receiving strength in His inner man.

Sitting down and celebrating is more than just taking a seat. It is about reflecting on what has been accomplished. It is about reward, praise and enjoying victories. Teachers understand this. In my former years as a school teacher, I loved attending our school graduation ceremonies and watching the excitement and satisfaction on the faces of the students as they were given awards. It is good for the soul when we are celebrated and appreciated. This is one of the reasons why birthdays will never go out of fashion or cease. They remind us that we are precious, and that we have something to be happy about.

Turning twenty-one is a big deal for us all. It is the year that signifies our transition into adulthood and independence. Fabulous parties with heart-warming speeches, music and dance as well as food are held in honour of the individual. It is a milestone. Parents respond with love, blessing and joy, ushering their children into adulthood. When I was at university my father was really struggling financially and it had been two years since my mother had passed away. When I turned twenty-one, my father could not afford a splashy birthday party for me — not even a small one. Nevertheless, I did treasure his wishes and fatherly words of blessing over me. I remember being at university the day of my twenty-first birthday feeling somewhat sad with no party and friends to celebrate my day. Unbeknownst to me, some of my student friends at university had organised a surprise twenty-first birthday party for me on campus. Wow! I was totally surprised and so overwhelmed at their effort that I literally cried. It was not a splashy or grand party, but nevertheless it meant so much to me. If any of them are reading this book, thank you again, guys. I have not forgotten.

Celebrating special occasions in our lives reminds us that we are more important than what we do. We ought to celebrate people for who they are more than what they do. Even if a person does not achieve any great success in life, they ought still to be celebrated. Heaven is going to be one big celebration in our honour. A new baby is received with great joy and love into the family. Well, we have been born into the family of God our Father and a huge celebration filled with joy and love awaits us!

God makes it a habit to commend us and reward us. Every good deed we do for others is as good as if we are doing it for God. Such good efforts are noted by God, as clearly stated in *Hebrews 6:10: "God is not unjust; He will not forget your work and the love you have shown Him as you help His people and continue to help them" (NIV).* There are so many heroes of the faith whose names we have never heard, but who are doing great exploits for God. One day in Heaven we will get to know them when God Himself celebrates their lives and rewards their good work done on earth. *"Therefore, my dear brothers and sisters … always give yourselves fully to the work of the Lord, because you know that your labour in the Lord is not in vain" (1 Corinthians 15:58, NIV).* There are no wasted efforts. They all count.

After Jesus completed His work on earth, He ascended into Heaven and sat at the right hand of God the Father. No one should work aimlessly without a target or goal in mind. That seated position Jesus took spoke of a completed work. It spoke of success. It spoke of a coming celebration. While we are left here on earth to continue the powerful ministry of Jesus, we are reminded in Scripture that our rest, celebration and reward time is on the way.

Rewards and joyous time await us in Heaven. God has a stupendous store of them waiting for us because He knows they will bless our hearts. It is in God's nature to commend and reward. There is going to be a grand and prestigious feast. God the Father, God the Son and God the Holy Spirit, along with the angels and twenty-four elders will be there. All the saints will be there. What a wonderful sight it will be. We are going to be dressed in the best outfits made in Heaven. We are going to have glorified bodies prepared for us by God. These bodies will never get sick or die. There are going to be crowns and mansions for us, not to mention streets of gold to walk on *(Revelation 21–22; John 14:2).* It is going to be a splashy celebration that will make all celebrations on earth look dim.

Paul gave us a glimpse into our coming Heavenly reward ceremony. He said, *"Finally, there is laid up for me a crown of righteousness, which the Lord, the righteous judge, will give me on that Day, and not to me only but also to all who have loved His appearing" (2 Timothy 4:8 NKJV).* The apostle Peter echoed this sentiment when he said, *"And when the Chief Shepherd [Jesus] appears, you will receive the crown of glory that does not fade away" (1 Peter 5:4 NKJV).*

When we get to Heaven we will experience rest from everything negative that opposed us on earth *(Deuteronomy 12:10)*. We will have rest from the Devil, rest from fear and strife, rest from sin, sickness and disease. We will have rest from addictions and from iniquities. We will have rest from tragedy and uncertainty. This kind of rest exists only where God is. Jesus left us His peace because He knew we would need it in a stressful and restless world where persecution is unavoidable, but in Heaven we will know and experience the fullness of rest forever.

Heaven is a place of rest. No country goes into celebration mode in the middle of a devastating war, but when the war is over, and their victory has come, that country engages in extravagant celebration. Victory brings joy and rest. That is why Jesus gave us power over sin, sickness and death. They are enemies at war with us. Death can no longer do what it was originally designed to: separate us from God. When we die we leave this earth and are ushered straight into the presence of the Lord. Death may kill this physical body, but God has an eternal one, fully upgraded, ready as a far better replacement.

When David wanted to build a house of rest for God's tabernacle, God forbade him to do so because David represented war, being a man of bloodshed *(1 Chronicles 28:1–8)*. God chose Solomon to build a house of rest for His presence, since Solomon was not a man of war and represented peace. This testifies to the fact that where God dwells peace and safety are found, not chaos and war. Total rest and security are found, and God wants us to experience this *(Isaiah 32:18, NIV)*.

God sits as King on His throne. He is sovereign and full of power. This King cannot be defeated. When we are in Heaven there will never be another feeling of fear or anxiety. We will never feel threatened or vulnerable. There will be no bad or tragic reports to crush our hearts with pain. Our King knows how to fight our battles, banish our enemies and let us enjoy the victory. There will be no adverse situations to taunt us. It will be blissful forever. Heaven is not about our fighting anything, but celebrating our King, and the many great things He has done for us.

There will be no toil in God's presence. We will not feel the need to prove our worth to Him as we are so often inclined to nowadays. We have His full approval. He already knows what we are worth —

the blood of Jesus. This was the only currency that could be used to make us acceptable in Heaven. Jesus did all the work and suffering on the cross, so we could enjoy rest and peace. There will be no room for sadness and fear. There will be no room for emptiness and lack.

Welcome to the greatest feast that God will hold for us, His children. It is simple; God is a rewarder *(Hebrews 11:6)*. It is going to be a joyous reunion! No one should miss this glorious Holy Ghost party. Make Jesus the Lord of your life and your Heavenly invitation will be secure.

Not too long from now, we will take our seats in Heaven and celebrate! I can just hear Jesus saying, "SIT DOWN AND CELEBRATE."

RECAP

- There are times when we just need to sit down, rest, recuperate and celebrate, like God did on the seventh day of Creation.
- If we do not rest, we will become stressed and burn out. Long hours and days of work can starve relationships.
- Sitting down and celebrating is more than just taking a seat. It is about reward and praise, reflecting on what we have accomplished and enjoying the victory.
- It is good for the soul when we are celebrated and appreciated.
- While we are left here on earth to continue the powerful ministry of Jesus, we are reminded in Scripture that our rest and celebration time is on the way. Through the comfort and help of the Holy Spirit we get to experience a taste of what is to come.
- When we get to Heaven we will experience absolute rest from everything negative that opposed us on earth *(Deuteronomy 12:10)*.
- When we are in Heaven we will never experience feelings of fear or anxiety.
- Heaven is not about our fighting anything, but celebrating our King, and the many great things He has done for us.
- Make Jesus the Lord of your life and your Heavenly invitation will be secure.
- Not too long from now, we will take our seats in Heaven and celebrate!

More About the Author

Aubrey Morris was born and raised in Durban, South Africa. He attended Edgewood University, where he graduated as a schoolteacher. He taught in three different schools; two in South Africa and one in Ireland. Popular among his peers and students, he has inspired youth and adults with his positive attitude to life, caring nature and belief in God.

He founded the Addington Christian Club (A.C.C.), and he has run choir and drama groups through which he has impacted youth. He has also developed his musical abilities, performing in concerts and church services.

He emigrated to Ireland in 2005, where he continued to teach, while undertaking studies in theology at Grace Bible School. He has grown into a seasoned teacher, preacher, motivational speaker and musician.

He has also been involved with community organizations such as NEWRY FOOD BANK, SOSAD, CONCERN and SPIRIT RADIO. He also oversees a Men's Group called MOMENTUM at Newry Christian Centre, as well as teaching theology in Newry Kingdom Living Bible School. He also leads the NCC worship band at Newry Christian Centre.

Aubrey serves on the WAKEUP board, a youth-building organization in Ireland, as well as supervising the WAKEUP BAND. He has also facilitated mission trips to Southern Africa.

Aubrey is married to Auriel Morris. They have two sons: Dillon and Levi. The family resides in Dundalk, Ireland.

Other Books by Aubrey Morris

THE POTENTIAL OF YOUR LIFE

The Potential of Your Life is a motivational book loaded with spiritual and practical insight to equip you and leave you passionate about life as you exercise your potential and live out your God-given purpose. It will help bring out the best in you as you discover your significance.

Available: authorhouse.com

WISDOM FOR LIFE 101

Wisdom for Life 101 comprises a hundred and one bite-sized messages on WISDOM, the MAIN (principal) thing in life. Wisdom is the seedbed from which we cultivate an effective, wholesome and meaningful life.

Available: authorhouse.com

Contact for the author is via the publisher.